THE WORLD ENGAGED

Other Wood Thrush Books Publications:

Universal Nature
Philosophical Fragments from the Writings
of John Burroughs
edited by Walt McLaughlin

Beautiful Like a Mayfly
essays by Walt Franklin

The Unexpected Trail
Taking on the 100 Mile Wilderness
a narrative by Walt McLaughlin

Barbless Hooks and Anchorholds
a narrative by Benjamin Green

River's Edge
A Fly-Fishing Realm
essays by Walt Franklin

Loon Wisdom
Sounding the Depths of Wildness
essays by Walt McLaughlin

The Wildness Beyond
A Wood Thrush Books Anthology
of Nature Writing

Go to woodthrushbooks.com
for a complete list of Wood Thrush Books titles

THE WORLD ENGAGED

An Anthology of Nature Writing

edited by

Walt McLaughlin

Wood Thrush Books

Published by Wood Thrush Books
                27 Maple Grove Estates
                Swanton, Vermont 05488

ISBN 978-0-9903343-5-4

Table Of Contents

Prose

Prose/Poetry

Poetry

Acknowledgements

"Winter Green" is from David Cavanagh's slender collection of poems, *Straddle*, reprinted with permission from the Irish publisher Salmon Poetry.

"Late Summer" is a prose piece from *Teaching Trout to Talk* – a meditation on the zen of small steam fly fishing, written by Stuart Bartow (RA Press, 2014).

"Everything I Needed to Know about the Truth, I Learned from a Tree" has been taken from *Until Only Silence Remains* – a book of essays published by Benjamin Green in 2014 under the imprint Patricks Point Press.

The essay "Green Fire: Homage to Leopold" has been lifted from Walt Franklin's book, *Beautiful Like a Mayfly* (Wood Thrush Books, 2015).

Two of Jeanne Shannon's poems have previously appeared elsewhere: "Those Terrorist Flowers" in *Adobe Walls* magazine, and "Tulip Tree Standing..." in *Clinch Mountain Review*.

"The Pipes of Pan" is from *Mythus Antiquus*, a slender volume of poetry letterset then released by Clarence Wolfshohl under the imprint El Grito del Lobo in 2009.

"All or Nothing" is from *Waiting* – one of the many volumes of poetry penned by t. kilgore splake.

Susan Cohen's "Why Whales Are Poems" first appeared in *The Greensboro Review*. It was then published, along with "How to Imitate a Birch Tree," in her second full-length collection of poems, *A Different Wakeful Animal* (Red Dragonfly Press, 2016).

Alan Caseline granted permission for three of his poems to be reprinted here: "Tamed by the Gentle Alone," "On the Lake Following Thunder" and "Retreat That Distances Darkness." They have been taken from his book, *64 Changes* (Foothills Publishing, 2015).

The prose piece "Green Stones," which was written by t. kilgore splake under the pen name Casey Brendan, first appeared in *Mosaic*, a newsletter from the Calumet Art Center.

Diane Jarvenpa's poem, "Swim This Life," first appeared in her book, *...swift, bright, drift...*, published last year by Red Dragonfly Press.

Thistlewords Press published Scott King's *Rice County Odonata Journal, Volume Two* in 2012. The excerpt reprinted here is called "Journal: Part Three" in that book.

 "Bloodroot," "Woodpecker" and "Susquehannock" have been extracted from Walt Franklin's most recent collection of poems: *Earthstars, Chanterelles, Destroying Angels* (Foothills Publishing, 2016).

"The Sleepwalker" previously appeared in *Everything That Becomes,* a collection of essays and poems written then released by William Weiss in 2008.

"How I Dream" is Freya Manfred's contribution to this anthology. It previously appeared in *Speak, Mother* – a collection of her poems published in 2015 by Red Dragonfly Press.

The poem "Canoeing Mississagua Creek" is from Tony Cosier's book, *Carillonneur* (Penumbra Press, 2012).

Stuart Bartow's "Moon Lust" first appeared in the literary magazine *Blueline*, before being reprinted in his poetry collection *Einstein's Lawn* (Dos Madres, 2015). "Tiger Moths" has been taken from another collection of his, *Questions for the Sphinx* (WordTech Editions, 2011).

The two poems by Vicki Graham, "Slake" and "Six Reveries on Shells," are from her poetry collection, *The Hummingbird's Tongue* (Red Dragonfly Press, 2014).

"Black Butterflies," "Snowstorm After Midnight" and "Lichen" are from Scott King's poetry collection, *All Graced in Green* (Thistlewords Press, 2011).

"Woods Wandering" is a chapter in Walt McLaughlin's most recent book, *Cultivating the Wildness Within*, released by Red Dragonfly Press.

Introduction

While wandering through the woods, miles from any road or settlement, I feel wildness emerging from somewhere deep within me. Then I wonder how many other hikers feel the same way during their outings. Surely I'm not alone in this. What about canoeists, cross-country skiers, hunters and fishermen? What about country walkers, birdwatchers, or those who lose themselves in the simple beauty of wildflowers? Surely they must feel it as well. Is it even possible to engage the natural world in a way that doesn't coax wildness to the surface? And what is this wildness but a deep connection with the earth itself, with this place in the universe that we call home?

Perhaps "wildness" isn't the right word for it – not the word most people would use to describe the way they feel when they connect to nature. But in wild moments we experience an epiphany, a coming to terms with some aspect of the world we had not noticed before, or had not allowed ourselves to fully explore. It is all too easy for us to stumble through the days as if in a haze, lost in our thoughts, not seeing or feeling the world immediately around us. Distracted. That's how most of us live our workaday lives most of the time. But every once in a while we stop what we're doing and look around with the eye of a poet, discerning scientist, or careful observer. Then suddenly the world comes alive.

The world. What are we talking about here? Is it the *real* world of human interaction that we inhabit, or the *natural* world? When you think about it, there's no difference between the two. We impose our buildings and infrastructure upon the world in which we live, certainly, but that doesn't change what it is. The world, and everything in it, is natural. There is nothing else. And when we really pay attention to our surroundings, this fact becomes self-evident.

Putting together this anthology has been more of an unconscious effort than a conscious one. I published *The Wildness Beyond* back in 2011. A few years after that, I figured it was time to publish another Wood Thrush Books anthology. But I had no plan to do so. Then Benjamin Green's book, *Until Only Silence Remains*, landed on my desk. The long essay on trees in it spurred me to action. From that point forward I started collecting work starting with the poem "Sleepwalker" by William Weiss, which resonated with the woods wanderer in me. More good nature writing came my way so I collected more work for a would-be anthology. Still I had no plan. Or perhaps I should say, I had no *theme*. Then late last summer Scott King at Red Dragonfly Press sent me books by several poets he had recently published, and that did it. I found myself gravitating to the poems in those books where a connection to the natural world was obvious, where the poet was feeling something akin to what I feel whenever I'm in the woods. Then I became acutely aware of my editorial bias. The rest was just a matter of saying "yes."

I have tried to be as open-minded as possible while making selections, including rather un-conventional writing along with the kind of poetry and prose that one would expect to find in a book like this. I have also selected work outside of my own comfort zone, simply because I felt the writer had something important to say in some new or interesting way. The result is, I hope, a collection of nature writing as diverse as nature itself. But I leave it to you, dear reader, to be the judge of that.

Walt McLaughlin
April 2017

THE WORLD ENGAGED

Bloodroot

I kneel at the cliffs
where a cream-white flower
glistens briefly in the sun.
Life at this altar lifts
greening from debris,
still fragile, tenuous,
at the mercy of frost
and wind. Palmate leaves
clasp the stem like hands
in prayer, waiting
for the call to unfurl
when sap flows red
in the root, when marrow
runs rich in the bone.

— Walt Franklin

A Day without Plastic

Through a tunnel of leaf-light
and swirling foam, downstream
beneath a canopy of mixed hemlock
and poplar, I work my way
to the next pool,

where square-tailed trout have merged
with the shadow of an overhanging ledge,
each breath, each thought,
each moment a mercurial shape
that strikes the surface

and then returns as suddenly
to its concealment. I look for tracks
in the silt, for the nearly
human-shaped hands of raccoons
which came in the night,

or for the bootprints of fishermen
who preceded me, even as I hope that
I am first on the brook today. If not
I resolve to carry solitude
within me

when I balance across a line of rocks
slick with spray. I wait for the morning
haze to clear, for a wood thrush
to sing among the leaves,
and for a dragonfly to alight

on my shoulder, causing an afterimage
when it darts away, its gauzy-thin
wings flickering in and out
of existence. Whenever I get dizzy
and can't catch my breath,

I stand perfectly still, picturing the earth
as it spins through space, protected
only by clouds. I give thanks
to gravity for keeping the world
from flying apart, and praise

the blood that courses through my veins
like the buzzing of bees thick
with pollen, or the unspoken
language of silence answering
all of my prayers

— Michael Jewell

Lichen

I'll try the trail again
in the evening after snowfall

like mist brushing bare winter branches
I'll become all that departs

I'll come quietly and linger
lean into trees   a kind of cloud

like the previous people who came as sparks
setting fires   only the fires went out

I'll drift like smoke into places
away from farms and cities

I'll be other than I imagine myself to be
as I look out on mink tracks on ice

ironwood trees   lichen living on rocks
I'll try to save this place

licking a slight taste from the land
becoming another anonymity

— Scott King

The Sleepwalker

There is a great distance
between me and life.
Sometimes I like to hike
all the way out there
you know set up camp
turn round and round
consternated at all
the critters trees breathe
and after a spell or two three
I've really no idea
where the hell I am
or how I came to be there.
So I sleep on it
toss and turn
on the bumpy earth
until I'm exhausted.
Finally I drop off
one eye open out of habit.
And it's the damndest thing.
When I wake up
I'm always back here.

— William Weiss

Neutral Colors

by Helen Ruggieri

Watched a show on the Home and Garden channel last night about a decorator's use of rust, beige, tan, gray and ecru providing a neutral background against which to display your objet d'art. On the way to work the fields speed by – rust, beige, tan, gray and ecru. Burnt sienna, ocher, cream, manila, last oak leaves, frost blown tops of goldenrod, giant reeds, wild grasses.

If you stretch a wire between two poles and pluck it, it will vibrate forever. Once a sound is made the vibrations never stop. All the sounds the world has made are out there floating in the atmosphere.

If you had the equipment you might hook up the electrical impulses of your brain to musical instruments and play them with your mind – the brain's music, EEG's, the electrical pulse of our thoughts surging through our neural pathways making a sax play "Love Me Tender."

I was walking the dog down by the river where ponds form in abandoned gravel pits. At dusk a flock of

Canada geese flew over us coming in low to settle onto the ponds. They were no more than six feet over my head, honking and braking with their wings, the leaders splashing into the pond. The last of the light made their white bellies ghostly glows. The dog was barking. The disrupted air from the many wings raised my hair the way static electricity tingles around you. Honking, barking, my pleasure cry, that music radiating forever in the atmosphere against the neutral noise, white noise, the unsorted background sounds of everyday against which joy stands out.

holding a shell
to my ear
my own music

Moon Lust

([S]pace is nothing. It has no existence and is not a reality... Space therefore exists only in relation to our particularizing consciousness.)
— The Tibetan Book of the Dead

Out for a walk one night, the moon
at his side, William Blake had an urge
to fling himself into it, never
to return. Legend has it that Li Po,
wine-drunk, leapt over the bow of a boat
to grasp the moon's reflection,
and drowned. Once submerged,
he must have continued to struggle,
to gather that perfect flower
above him. One night
a star will drift closer and closer.
You will reach for it and, as space vanishes,
you will touch that orb, and disappear.

— Stuart Bartow

Why Whales Are Poems

They see things their own way.
I imagine they have philosophies,

and some are arrogant, but they can do
little harm without opposable thumbs.

As long as whales are, the story is larger
than us, too big for prose.

Useless to ask a whale what it means. It's shapely
and precise, but we will never translate it.

Their bodies, undivided, tempt
barnacles and other flagrant scribblers.

Because whales break the water open, shift
ocean and sky, sing their adumbrated songs,

carry their own light and shade.
Because they amplify.

— Susan Cohen

Retreat That Distances Darkness

not passing moods
caught between withdrawals
equinox nears
when light
overtakes the dark

fitful ground
no sign of growth

wind fallen
flood collected

bare maple branches
brown pine needles

sweeping storm
would wash these away
roots thought secure
need a hold
to stay and endure

tears carried away in floods
fled desperate struggles
keep distance
inaccessible as heaven

— Alan Caseline

The Wild in Your Own Back Yard

by Richard Aston

We enjoy the wild in our back yard by not cutting the grass in Spring until we can mow around flowers sprouting from weeds to honor Robert Frost's admonition, in his poem "The Tuft of Flowers", to let the "bloom the scythe has spared" be. Early last June, a charmingly hesitant young neighbor lady who asked me when I was going to cut the weeds had a point; the yard looked unkempt. But by July we were able to illustrate another style for her, as we had done enough cutting around the plants to set them off for special view. The process of selection and framing yielded profuse pleasure and surprise, as for example, when Milkweed produced a delicate flower, yellowish in flat umbels that open in the morning and disappear most of the day; which we photographed, just in case, to prove to the authorities that the cluster in the front yard blooms and is not a weed as prohibited by our city's ordinance.

Other free, often indigenous flowers, in my amateur opinion, that have dropped into our yard, as described in R. T. Peterson's *Field Guide to Wildflowers of Northeastern America*, provide a display of bloom throughout the summer, new species putting out flowers at different times as others fade. Among the first are common blue violets and the yellow flowers of dandelion in early spring. Soon after Daisy Fleabane shows off white to violet ray pedals, enhancing a yellow center, lasting into mid July. Also, English Plantain appears with clusters of tiny greenish white flowers persistent through the summer, that even pop back up after you mow them. Indian Strawberry-like fruit trails along the grass so that the mower can pass over. If only your typical lawn mower could be raised above four inches, sparing them would be easier. In June wild raspberries, which form a bramble behind our garage yield tasty fruit if you pick it within a week of its peak of ripeness. In mid summer, Day Lily produces showy three and a half inch yellow-orange blooms from June through July. Just a couple of weeks later, Swamp Rose-Mallow, commonly called Rose of Sharon blooms; and this woody plant is especially hearty and prolific, yielding showy two to three inch flowers. Nearing August, Peppermint comes with pale violet flowers and emits a familiar aroma for your added pleasure. Then by late summer Field Sow Thistle blooms and Great Burdock produces grooved, reddish purple-like flowers, which turn to burrs in the fall that hitch a ride by sticking to your clothing. Occasionally a sunflower pops up in unexpected places, from seed dropped by birds feeding on last year's planted stand. Pokeweed sprouts a large plant growing, by September, stalks up to ten feet high and yielding clusters of purple fruit which is toxic, but not deadly, according to the internet, even if you eat as much as you can of that bitter-tasting fruit, unless it is injected. Another large species, an eight foot high stand of milkweed teems up with Morning Glory vines entwined around it for decoration, and surprises us with a tower of bloom into Fall.

This profuse diversity is enhanced because we live less than a half mile from the Susquehanna River on soil made fertile by flood waters, last climbing seven feet up our living room walls in June 1972. (The dike has been raised to prevent this inconvenient triumph of the wild again for 500 years, hopefully.) These plants provide a symphony of color and form by blooming at different times during the summer, producing flowers from so small it helps to have a magnifying glass to view them, to showy specimens several inches across, and all free. For sure, buzzing bees, bright butterflies, brilliant birds, meandering moths, and innumerable insects show by their frequent visitation that they appreciate these.

As E. O. Wilson says, our impulse to cut weeds and kill bugs is just the kind of ordinary behavior we are beginning to realize is to our own detriment, setting us up for ecological collapse, following from the artificial niche of huge houses, automobiles, and golf-course-like manicured lawns we have built around ourselves.

Wavefield

Four rows of low, grassy hills.

Each one precisely formed,
graduated, rising, emulating waves.

Static landscape, mimicking
the sea.

— Alan Catlin

Early Morning in the Mist

by Helen Ruggieri

Like being in a large bowl, the hills, glaciated, unglaciated, making a ragged edge. Always a bank of clouds rising over them when the weather turns. Sometimes the cloud cover is so low that the car barely has enough room to squeeze through underneath. If I stopped, I could climb on the roof and haul myself up, run across the tops of the hills, valley and ridge, valley and ridge. Rise and dive, rise and dive.

Girl
(why not)
on a dolphin

Tulip Tree Standing in the North Fork of the Powell River Appalachia, Virginia

Sometimes a tree tells you more than can be read in books
— C. G. Jung

Tulip tree: A tall, deciduous, eastern North American tree,
Liriodendron tulipifera, *of the Magnolia family, having
large tulip-like green and orange flowers, aromatic twigs,
and yellowish, easily worked wood.*

Stalwart amid broken rocks in the center of the river, the
restless and unforgiving river, carrying its dank cargoes of
mud and human trash.

Stunted and small, assaulted endlessly by winds and
stinging weathers. At the mercy of a waterfall that shows
no mercy.

Sometimes a log washes against it, bending it double, but
when the log is gone it straightens and stands up again.

It cannot grow into its tall cone shape. It cannot open its
orange goblet-flowers, nor welcome birds to nest among its
branches. How lonely it seems, how mute and solitary,
under the glow of western sunsets, season after season.

When its sister trees along the riverbank break out in
fragrant tulip blooms, what does it whisper on the wind?

*(With thanks to Howard E. Cummins for his article "A Tree
Grows in Appalachia," in the Big Stone Gap, Virginia* Post.*)*

— Jeanne Shannon

Winter Green

The green grass of January
shocks softly, warns
even as it cheers,
more news than the news,
cracks a frigid smile.

— David Cavanagh

Slake

Heat and drought. Brittle,
the forest is thirsty, on the edge of fire.

Listen: the river curls over stone
all night. Wind lifts the branches
of the firs, and an owl calls
once, twice, falls silent.
What can a garden do to assuage longing
for home? What can soil and seed
offer the wandering heart?

To live in cut gem minimalism,
a life of bleached stone.
But a garden must have water.

— Vicki Graham

All or Nothing

in the desert — man is there
god is not   blazac

few people find
sacred spiritual feelings
abundant in desert space
preferring holy book passages
religious scripture words
for explanations of life
thousands of years passing
rainwater melting ice and snow
creating brilliant red landscape
massive buttes and mesas
glowing like fiery forge
moments of creation
before bethlehem manger
time of eden
sandstone petroglyphs
describing native magic
rolling piling while clouds
becoming black thunderheads
wild mustangs racing across plains
dust devils blowing through sand
today shadowy ghosts

still staring at heavens
celebrating gods
forgotten by others

— t kilgore splake

Bucophilia

by Helen Ruggieri

Bucophilia is the feeling we get when we look at a landscape that moves us – we say – oh, that's beautiful, but it's only hills and valleys and trees like everywhere else. How do we know beauty? We are connected to it by nostalgia, a feeling of connectedness, a longing for something long ago or far away, something pulling at us and we recognize it as beautiful.

And the opposite, the dread and horror, the anger at destruction, as when the highway crew building the new expressway dug in to the side of the hill and took out gravel to even the roadbed leaving the hill as if some monstrous Godzilla had taken a bite. Later they came and evened it out, planted some sticks that would be trees if they survived the harsh winter, but the shape of the hill, how it moved symmetrically down to the hollow to meet the upswelling of the next hill – that was gone. It was a memory, some nostalgic memory, how beauty and ugliness are connected in our mind, how we lose the connection with the earth and take one for another.

> in the hollow
> run off feeds a small stream
> leeks grow in spring

The Pipes of Pan

naked in the meadow
straight as would want to be
with timbrels and reeds
swirling sounds into arabesques

i dance in a frantic circle
outlined by familiar elders

outside the window the old goatman
sidles down the street
his whistle lingers
long after him

such a jig
only he could give me

such a wildness
the old folks fear

such a lust
the vigilant hide

such a sound
only the rocks can bare

— Clarence Wolfshohl

42

Green Fire: Homage to Leopold

by Walt Franklin

Our plane landed in El Paso with a midnight wind and a temperature of 100 degrees. Headed for Alamogordo, New Mexico, we braced ourselves for drought and summer weather unusual even by southwestern standards. Forest fires had already raged across western Arizona and northern New Mexico and at the moment were flaring up in the Sacramento Mountains near Alamogordo. We'd be staying with my wife's family on the outskirts of the city, but I was anxious to explore a cooler, wetter environment, hopefully north of Santa Fe. We'd learn that northern fires had forced the closure of public lands, so my wife and I began to look south and west. The Gila National Forest would be dry but green, remote and distant, and unknown by both of us. With the blessings of my father-in-law and his wife Terry, we departed from White Sands and the Tularosa Basin and drove to Glenwood, New Mexico near the Arizona border.

  En route to the Gila I observed, ever so briefly, my first life-bird on this journey from New York – my first sighting of a Harris hawk, soaring over Interstate 10 near Deming, New Mexico. The raptor's diagnostic trait was a chestnut coloration underneath its gliding body. We'd reserved a homestead cabin for three nights and would face the Mogollon Mountains and the Gila Wilderness. The renowned Catwalk National Historic Trail would be several miles up the road at Whitewater Canyon, and there I'd look for trout and wander through a birding wonderland where some 300 species of avian life could be found in a typical year.

The Gila was the nation's first designated wilderness, thanks to the early efforts of the pioneering author and conservationist, Aldo Leopold. The Gila, along with the adjacent Aldo Leopold and Blue wilderness regions, comprises much of a national forest system that includes one of the largest roadless areas in the Lower 48 states. Although the grizzly bear no longer roams the wilderness here, the Mexican gray wolf has been reintroduced, and bighorn sheep roam the higher altitudes. At first I was disappointed not to be cutthroat fishing and exploring in the Rockies north of Santa Fe, but I was starting to look forward to immersing myself in the Mogollons – at the southern rim of the trout's world in North America.

Following my purchase of a five-day fishing license at the general store in Glenwood (uncertain if I'd find enough water to actually fish in), we settled into our cabin grounds on a well-established ranch. Shortly afterward I found my second life-bird of the trip, the phainopepla, which resembles a big dark waxwing in profile, but with white wing-patches. It demonstrated a familiar flycatcher habit as it reeled gracefully from a treetop to snatch a flying insect.

Glenwood village is a small oasis in a valley with some wild American history and authentic airs. Several hundred residents host a bar, a few tourist shops and a general store, and give the visitor a base for rest and exploration. Our cabin site, one of several buildings on the ranch, was tucked against a rugged westward slope. Its air-conditioned rooms and modern amenities were a luxury not to be taken for granted. Although the hot Mexican climate could be brutal here throughout a summer day, the air is typically comfortable at night. The mountain air, and its smell, so difficult to define, was sweet no matter the hour, especially at our doorway with its table and chairs.

It was interesting to learn that the native Gila trout, one of the rarest of salmonids, was recently moved from the nation's Endangered List to that of Threatened status, thanks to the work of the Federal Gila Trout Recovery Team and its support groups. The Gila could now be fished for in select recovery streams, under special regulations. In another season, with more time for hiking into the remote canyons, it would be fun to fly-fish for this beautiful trout. For now, however, I was satisfied attempting to locate the more accessible hybrid species, the Gila-rainbow, in nearby Whitewater Creek.

Shortly after our arrival in Glenwood, Leighanne and I inspected the mouth of Whitewater Canyon where the Catwalk Trail begins and where the sycamores introduce a fascinating riparian zone. Storm clouds were brewing slowly over the Mogollons, and thunder rolled down the canyon slopes as if to announce commencement of the monsoon rains – none too soon, according to local residents. Parts of New Mexico hadn't seen rain in nine or 10 months. The first raindrops puddled on the dry creek bed, on the parking lot and on the hardpan roadside as we drove back to the cabin. Polly, our hostess, welcomed our arrival with hearty thanks for "bringing on" the first brief shower. With the smell of desert rain, one could almost hear the floral pores of creosote plants opening to grasp new moisture in the air. When these desert plants embrace the moisture they release a famous odor, one of my favorite southwestern sensations.

After an early morning walk near the cabin, viewing birds such as black-headed grosbeak, Say's phoebe, and acorn woodpecker, Leighanne and I visited the canyon. Among the first visitors for the day, we entered the mountains via the Catwalk, an excellent suspension trail that follows a historic pipeline path once used by silver mine employees from a mill that had been located near the present day parking lot. The Catwalk leads upstream through the canyon for more than a mile, at an average height of 10 to 20 feet above the Whitewater. Thankfully the creek, although intermittent for a while near the parking lot, had water in it – a cold, clear flow that strengthened as we walked. And pleasantly enough, the eye of this fly-fisher caught the sight of trout. Small quick motions in the limpid flow counter-balanced the rise of canyon walls, the heights of which were staggering.

Although the native Gila trout had been nearly exterminated in the 1900s through habitat destruction and the stocking of rainbow trout (with which the Gila readily interbreeds), the hybrid flourished below the Catwalk. Stalking with a fly rod I could wet-wade into the tails of Whitewater pools and catch them on a dry fly. The small yellowish trout were darkly spotted on their olive backs and had the parr markings of a rainbow. I released them in quick succession from the barbless stonefly pattern and returned them to their haunts. By observing wild creatures of the region – the mule deer, lizards, insects, and especially the birds and trout – I felt capable of entering the landscape and gaining access to its spirit in the best way possible, considering the limits of our time, money and physical ability. By doing so, I also tried to acknowledge the impact that Aldo Leopold, author of *A Sand County Almanac* and of essays expressing the new American land ethic, had on modern life.

High above the "Swimming Hole," a well-oxygenated trout pool formed by a narrow waterfall, we saw numerous white-throated swifts flying near their nesting sites in zigzag patterns. Leighanne suggested that these rapid fliers at the canyon walls were mocking my attempts to identify bird notes and to link them with their species of origin. I refuted the possibility, saying the swifts couldn't care less about slow-walking hominids of the canyon. These swifts were reputed to be the fastest birds in North America, attaining speeds of close to 200 miles per hour. Whatever issues a flying swift might have with tourists, the bird passed them by so quickly as to be non-existent.

In thinking about the Gila country, I recalled the Native American novelist N. Scott Momaday, whose work I enjoyed reading many years ago. Momaday had said, "Once in his life a man ought to give himself up to a particular landscape in his experience; to look at it from as many angles as he can, to wonder upon it; to dwell upon it."

The Gila wasn't my "remembered earth." The country was new to me and I was getting introduced. It was all immediacy and presence, but there was something personal and familiar with the way that birds winged across my life in this locale, with the way that trout swam from the canyon waters into my blood, because I had sought them as of old. I met them in the wild, and for that the Gila wouldn't be forgotten. Still, our time here was short; I tried to concentrate intently on the place, and looked to see it from as many angles as I could.

Strolling near the cabin on a national forest road I trained binoculars on a red bird, a tanager. Again it was the summer tanager. I was hoping to find the similar hepatic tanager, with its darker cheek and bill, a species that would be a life-bird for me. Waiting on birds, I met a cowboy on a horse.

The young horseback rider paused for me as our trails converged. The fellow pushed a cowboy hat from his brow, spat tobacco juice from his mouth, and explained that he was a rancher just riding over the mountain. He spoke softly and slowly and directed as many words to his chestnut mare as he did to me. A sheathed rifle was slung to his saddle. He had been a rancher and a truck driver living near Artesia, but trying to make amends with his separated wife, he relocated to the Glenwood area. He seemed to approximate my stereotype of the Western cowboy in almost every way but one—his leisure time.

He told me he'd been riding over backcountry trails today, not exactly hunting or herding cattle, but simply trekking through the Gila out behind the Whitewater, higher up than anywhere I could go in my limited time. Referring to the canyon lands well above the Catwalk Trail, he described what he had seen: "The country is real pretty."

Thus I longed to know more. What about those canyons and those mesas he had seen or crossed? All I saw was vastness, vague and undefined. Roughly speaking, the Gila is a wilderness block about 100 miles north and south by 60 miles east and west in one of the remotest regions of the continental United States. There was no way I could know it well in a lifetime, let alone in four short days. So I begged apology to the frailty of the human condition, and thanked the modern cowboy for his words.

A short time after, while drinking Mexican beer at our cabin porch, I spotted life-birds number three and four, the band-tailed dove and the gray-breasted jay. They were right in front of me in the shrubbery by the driveway. Like the big green lizard that ran across the stones to perch on a standing log, the birds were emissaries of the Gila, and together they served the country to the visitor like a waiter serving a plate.

The next morning, following the latest life-bird sighting (a Cassin's sparrow), we got another early start on the Catwalk. Where I'd previously seen a sizeable trout beneath a log in a small pool near the picnic area, I made a single cast and caught a 10-inch rainbow. In a second pool beneath a water chute upstream, I caught another trout with a singular bow cast. Okay, I thought, so where's the challenge? It would come soon enough.

At one point, boulders in the creek bed braided the flow and helped create a series of enchanting pools. I descended to a couple of the pools and started casting from my knees. The colorful hybrids rose fearlessly to the artificial, and again I quit after releasing my fifteenth or sixteenth trout of the day. With that, Leighanne and I hiked on. It was the onset of a holiday weekend and the increase in the number of trail walkers was becoming painfully obvious.

I stopped to pull half a dozen discarded water bottles from the creek, and once again cursed the mind-set of those who were callous to the beauty of the land. As if to reward my good deed for the day, we were visited briefly by life-bird number six: a painted redstart that had perched in a short tree just a few feet off the trail. The bird was unmistakable with its patented red breast and black head. I saw white patches on the wings and tail. I had read that this "uncommon summer resident" of the Gila Canyonlands could be found near oak trees at an elevation between 5000 and 8000 feet. I'd been ready for this colorful creature, but discovering it was special nonetheless.

North of Glenwood is a place called Alma, population 10. We turned right at the Alma junction and proceeded eastward on a dusty corrugated road past broken trailer homes and ranches, stopping six miles later where the road dead-ended at a wooden corral. That's where Cooney Canyon opened to the valley. Cooney was named for an early gold seeker who was buried nearby. It is the lesser twin of Whitewater Canyon, if by "lesser" we mean that it's slightly smaller, maybe wilder and less visited by tourists. Like the Whitewater, Cooney is a slot canyon formed by water in the Mogollons, although today its formative agent, Mineral Creek, was dry and gone – at least in its lower end.

Standing in the lower canyon, we were probably the only humans for miles around. We were like the lost spirit of Mineral Creek except for the assurance that water could be found higher in the canyon if we ventured far enough. We listened to thunder cracking and rumbling from the peaks above, and rain was starting to patter on rocks and dust.

I had read that Mineral Creek was a place to visit if you wanted "peace, quiet, and a chance to fish for small trout." But again our timing was less than ideal. The rock columns in the canyon were spectacular, their sculpture forming a "pink box canyon." But the knife-blade edges and rectangular formations had an alien feel about them as I linked the stone and washed-out trail to the possibility of a flash flood from the storms beyond.

It was possible to climb into the canyon for a couple of miles and find a concrete remnant of the gold-mining town called Cooney. The allure was palpable but, for me at least, the desert rain made the jumbled stream bed seem foreboding. This was Billy the Kid and Butch Cassidy terrain, the place where Cooney's scalp met the Apache blade, and I was wimping out, according to my wife who's usually right about these matters. Blame it on the rain or blame it on my cowardice, my quiet walk behind Leighanne through Cooney Canyon was a futile attempt to "think like a mountain" as Aldo Leopold might do.

We found a secluded canyon seep, a mossy dooryard to a spring suggesting that water wasn't far away. But when would Mineral Creek appear? There were miles of canyon to ascend, with a couple of side trails dropping into the higher reaches from the small road above Mogollon village, but we would never see them.

We had visited Mogollon earlier. The village is a regionally famous "ghost-town" high up on the Whitewater Mesa, and we'd gotten there with a winding nine-mile climb while hugging the cliffs at 20 miles per hour. Its days of hosting 14 saloons during the gold and silver-mining era are long gone and replaced now with a modest display of artisans' gallery, antique shop, museum, and café.

The dark stillness of the canyon was interrupted by occasional voices, by the rocky syllables of thunder, and by avian notes from canyon wren, black phoebe and summer tanager. We stood in obeisance to the eerie quiet or else attempted to capture or comprehend the wildness by taking a photograph. Mineral Creek, however, was beyond us in another season or upon another level, gone within the leaves of sycamore or the otherworldly forms of rock. Its trout, the black-spotted yellowish hybrids, were relegated to imagination. I would learn that the canyon had been a candidate site for Gila trout reintroduction back in 1994, but the plan by the Recovery Team had been dashed by opposition from officials here in Catron County. The way I saw it, the loss was the county's, first and foremost.

We saw a starved black horse shuffling along in search for something edible left behind by free-roaming cattle. Its black ribs were obvious as a bleached bone on the desert floor, and its ghost of a rider was the history of human penetration into the canyons of the Gila. As we passed the black horse on the Cooney Canyon Road, we noticed that the rain had stopped and the domineering sun had reappeared.

With our early morning departure from the Glenwood cabin we paused to listen to a chorus of coyotes from across the roadway. The cacophony of yips and cries reminded us of kids shouting and screaming. The coyotes, neither pleased nor sorry to see us leave the area, had their own agenda for the edge of Gila country. I wondered how far inside the wilderness their larger cousins, the Mexican gray wolves, might be found. Hopefully they were doing fine despite the hardship faced through forest fires and an element of unsupportive cattle ranchers in the state. The wolves, recently reintroduced to their native southwestern habitat, deserved their rank in the food chain and their place among the elk and mule deer populations. If cattlemen, pushing their herds through public lands along the Gila's edge, grew an extra cow or two for the wolf each year, they would probably do everyone a favor.

I thought of the gray wolf as we stopped at Aldo Leopold Vista off the highway south of Glenwood. There, in the solitude of arid ground dedicated to the great twentieth-century environmentalist and writer, a jackrabbit hopped into shade of a pinyon pine, and a family of Gambel's quail scurried for cover. A low plaque in front of us identified the mountains and canyons to the east. We saw an interface of desert and mountain worlds, an edge to our visual realm and the point from which imagination was required to make contact with the vastness of the Gila. The view we had was excellent by virtue of the land just being there for its own sake, and secondarily for whatever non-destructive pleasures that people could derive from it. This was wilderness protected by law, the country's first designated wild place, thanks to the early efforts of Aldo Leopold, a forest supervisor for the Gila. The youthful Leopold was less than fond of wolves.

Leopold shared a belief common to his time. The big predators in the southwestern food chain, the mountain lion and the wolf, were detrimental to the populations of deer and elk that sportsmen liked to hunt. As a hunter himself, Leopold freely targeted what the ranchers and hunters wanted removed. One day, after shooting into a pack of wolves with cubs, he caught up with several wounded animals. In the eyes of a dying she-wolf he observed the slow ebb of a "fierce green fire" that would later symbolize for him the glory of wild nature. The banked green fire in the gray wolf's eyes would mark him deeply in the years to come. It would change not only Leopold's opinion about the role of wolves and predators; it also revolutionized his view of nature and the balance of life.

Leopold's evolving career as a conservationist, educator, and author led him into studies far and wide. The "land ethic" that he helped formulate was one he lived by and promoted intensely. His impact on our culture is incalculable. I felt his guidance strongly when I settled in an old farmhouse many years ago.

At Silver City we climbed a small road north into the ponderosa forest. Two hours, or 45 miles later, we arrived at Gila Cliff Dwellings National Monument. The road had been a jeep trail until recent decades but the land on every side remained remote and wild. Life-bird number seven flew across my view as we proceeded. A red-faced warbler suggested that identification is easy at times – if you've planned for the possibilities to be found in each new setting. A good field guide is essential.

Fire had razed the forest only weeks ago. The so-called Miller Fire had burned through a hundred thousand acres of national forest, its blaze apparently caused by human carelessness. Even near the Visitors' Center we could smell the charred remains. But what surprised us was the green growth already pushing outward into the sun, the leaves and stems energizing from blackened stumps and roots. It was the fierce green fire of the Gila – the wildness banked and endlessly reborn.

The scene was like the "Mesa of the Angels" known to Leopold. This was dry Apache land, angular and sharp. The Gila River edges were threaded with cottonwood, sycamore and willow. Meadows were spangled with penstemon, and the canyon seeps with columbine. Here I found the deep enchantment. We had dropped down from the ponderosa pine. The high desert had eased us through the pinyon and juniper. And here the Gila with its three-pronged origins flowed beyond our comprehension. We could try to reach for an understanding of the watershed, but it was more important to relax and wallow in the moment.

We were greeted by park volunteers and then strolled upward through the leafy Cliff Dwellers' Canyon. When the trail turned sharply from a stream it followed, we got our first view – deep caves along the south-facing slope. The series of side-by-side caves reflected quiet voices of a group of visitors, words echoing perfectly in natural acoustics of the place. In the first cave I imagined a tribal sound of beating drums, of ceremonial rhythms in thirteenth-century Mogollon life, of human habitation in multi-structured caves.

We climbed stairs and ladders, learning of pre-Mogollon peoples here, and of those who would come later – the Apaches, followed by nineteenth-century white explorers, many of whom pilfered and destroyed the vestiges. A sympathetic tourist could marvel at the prospect of a home range set inside a beautiful canyon, at the certain harshness that primitive life must have known here. Settlements were of short duration, less than a lifetime in some cases. They were at the mercies of climate and human enemies despite the ideal remoteness. Today the dwellings shone in late-morning sun but also sheltered their own dark mysteries. In the canyon below the caves we could see the streaked remains of the recent Miller Fire. Since half of the circuit trail to the dwellings had been closed because of the fire, we descended by the same route we had climbed. It was an odd thing: the home range of the cave dwellers seemed worlds away from where we lived today, and yet it felt close enough beneath our skins that we could almost touch it.

Aldo Leopold eventually moved to Wisconsin to work and live, espousing the virtues of self-reliance and independence. He bought an old farm whose refurbished "shack" became the center for his inspirations. There he witnessed his place as a microcosm for earth, a living entity "vastly less alive than ourselves in degree, but vastly greater than ourselves in time and space." His book *A Sand County Almanac and Sketches Here and There* was published posthumously in 1948 and would soon be recognized as an environmental classic. The book's portrayal of a personal "home range" would inspire thousands of back-to-the-land enthusiasts (including myself) in the decades to come. The Leopold ideals of beauty, tolerance and respect were adopted slowly by many people of the later twentieth-century.

The Leopold life was one of courage and conviction. He evolved from being an effective and utilitarian manager of southwestern forests and wildlife into a crusader for the scientific preservation of American wilderness. The land ethic he developed and promoted is a reverence to the principles of ecology. As a conservationist and educator, Leopold adhered to the belief that land comprises a community of interacting lives. It is not a singular commodity designed merely for man's consumption or manipulation. According to Leopold, to discover what makes land healthy and stable, all we have to do is roam across our rural districts with our senses on alert. We'd do well to explore our watersheds and forestlands, our home place, and to study neglected species in all seasons. We should stay in touch with wilderness and listen to the howl and cry of predator and prey.

Every part of the land is good, said Leopold, whether we understand what we see or not. We're an element of the land; our job as citizens is to learn about the natural world we live in and to act accordingly – to respect the green fire burning gently through each life.

Leighanne wanted a quick inspection of the Visitors' Center. We were scheduled to return to Alamogordo later in the day; our time was running short. Leighanne dropped me off at the trailhead close to the Middle Fork Gila River and the Visitors' Center. She would join me later.

My first choice for fishing was the West Fork Gila, flowing near the Cliff Dwellings, but its water was low because of the drought. The Middle Fork looked tempting – if I could find water cold enough for trout. The upstream hike was hot beneath a midday sun.

I crossed the river in my shorts and sandals, and the water felt tepid. In the shade of a rare cottonwood tree I rigged the three-piece fly rod and then proceeded for half a mile. The canyon walls echoed with birdsong even at this late hour. I heard orioles, thrashers and wrens. High on the west cliff was a cave that looked inaccessible. I wondered if it was the cave where explorers had found a mummified child and later donated the discovery to the Smithsonian Institute. But this was no time for distractions. Given the time constraints I had to focus on the river.

A small stone-lined spring entered from the east. I thought it might be a shot of cold water to enliven my prospects for trout. I stuck my hand into the flow and pulled it back in record time. Cold water? No, scalding water! I was surprised it wasn't boiling.

Upstream of the hot stuff the river felt icy by comparison. A large fish rolled at the surface near a bank. It may have been a carp. Beyond it was a deep, calm pool, and I laid a dry fly on its surface. A fish struck, and I missed it. Then another struck at the imitation, but the hook-up was a short one. The missed opportunity repeated itself several times and I knew that something was awry. The river's green zone had become rather lush; the hiking trail was indistinct. Maybe it was time to meet Leighanne back at the cottonwood.

The renowned fly-fisher Arnold Gingrich once wrote, "A trout is a moment of beauty known only to those who seek it." In my search for a Middle Fork trout I knew some moments of beauty *before* a fish was found. I was skunked by the Gila but my effort at fishing got rewarded with something other than trout. I saw that the link between an old streamwalker and the wilderness was strong. If I could speak of it simply, I would say that the connection was fun to wade through. I might also think of it as an "Aldo Leopold thing."

Introducing a Crocus Blossom

First up
   in the lavender and yellow Spring
I reach   for it in the blooming
      moist earth.
Just one Crocus   all by itself
    yet there will be more
in the border of lawn,
    more pushing upwards
to greet the new warmth
             of the sun, the sun greedy to see
what its days can make
    now
that it has come closer to earth. Winter snow
can no longer linger next to the authority
of those petals.
Crocus, a miniature flower
    but not one to go unnoticed
surrounded as it is
    by daffodils
not yet
    born.

— Karen McKinnon

Canoeing Mississagua Creek
(Rideau Lakes)

We make for pickerel weed on the paddle side
And, grazing the tips of the floating lanceheads, swing
To where the left bank swerves and sickles wide
And draws us into a new meandering.

Curve on curve as we skim the changing edge
Vegetation and earth and water share each arc,
As mermaid's hair in sinuous strands submerged
Sways with surface lilies in the undulant creek.

And so our love across long years moves on,
Evolves, finds breathing room in subtle pivoting,
Explores new ground with gradual transformation,
Keeping a keel as constant as gravity.

— Tony Cosier

Realization

When I hunted Hinschkens' fields,
sitting the edge, facing
into this pocket, into woods and swamp,
standing corn behind –
a sudden cracking to my left.
Then it's there

like it's never yet been,
or always was coming,
steaming chuffing, tongue
curled up to reach outstretched
nose, neck so fat, monstrous
bull-ready for any

encounter, rack with so many or
some or a few points, I don't know:
How many do you really count
when you see the whole great thing
coming at you, gray river
flowing through the trees

in a cloud of November mist?
So I nock an arrow and sit
and watch the buck pass
not 10 yards in front of me
crunching rime ice.

— Gene Grabiner

Flashes

by William Weiss

All As It Should Be

In the end, all that will be left will be cocky ravens, crabby cacti, toxic encampments of datura, skinny mice farting deadly hanta virus, dozing diamondbacks waiting for a live one, giant hairy desert scorpions, scowling Indians, and crazy mystics hallucinating from spoiled government cheese in dilapidated trailers. Which is all as it should be.

Petroglyphs

Death Valley is a godforsaken wasteland, mottled, boulder-strewn, fabulously empty, forbidden. At night the sky is crowded, aglow with the distant campfires of the dead. After a long day of hiking in ridiculous heat he rounded a bouldered corner and sat down tired on a large, flat rock. He took a long drink of lukewarm water and lit up a joint. The sun was falling in the west. It was

66

better than pretty. Military aircraft boomed overhead and he turned his head to follow them. Behind him was a 50' cliff wall ablaze in reflected sunset. Petroglyphs were writhing there, as if alive. It's hard to imagine that there was a time when living in Death Valley was actually possible. In petroglyphs, there are two phases of graphic depictions of antlered animals, one in strict profile with the antlers curving back, and one straight-on, with the antlers branching out left and right. The latter orientation is the later style, and that's what he had found. No human is hunting in Death Valley anymore, except maybe biologists fretting over the fate of the several thousand different species of life that hold out there, many of which can't be found anywhere else. The southwest has become progressively drier over the last 10,000 years. America is turning into desert faster than Africa, and carbon-powered climate change is not helping.

Jack's Canyon

It's the elk he tracked outside of Flagstaff on the Kaibab Plateau. It's the elk he surprised one morning in Jack's Canyon, six of them, with a magnificent stag on point. He had gotten his breakfast fire started only a few minutes earlier when 80 yards from him in the timber, the six started coming down. He'd seen lots of tracks in the same spot the day before, it was a crossing,

so he set up his little camp in a bend in the canyon wall
with vantage of it in mind. The stag got 2/3rds of the
way down the canyonside before he spotted the
campfire – he was upwind, he couldn't smell it. At
once, as if one animal, the six of them turned and tore
up the hill through the pines. He wasn't hunting, but if
he had been, he'd have had time to get off one good
shot, but only one, that's how fast they were.

Boom Boom Boom

We hiked in a light spring rain and a field of beech
being made lacy green light suffusing the slopes which
are switchbacked, nicely switchbacked, switchbacked
and not slippery at all. Translucent orange salamanders
crept everywhere up and down, somnolent and sure
sure sure. Quartz, garnet and sand dripping. Jack in the
Pulpits dripping. White trillium and shooting fern
dripping. Green frog, red frog, black frog leaping. The
stream grew and grew and wherever the trail drew near
it made talk hard, which was good. At one point, the
stream broke into 3 falls, rushed its cut channels, fell
among rocks and boulders, dropped a clean and cold 20
feet. He clambered up surefooted in boots, his pack
clacked against rock and cataract ruckus, took off his
cap, stuck his head in that water and just as quick took
it out and shook long hair happy as a dog. The close
cold soaked quick into his sweatshirt. He looked down

at his friends and in just that moment, in a shiver and a shiver, everything was so real he thought he might die. It happens that way sometimes, you know. You are far below the dam and whistling and roaming the riverbed when suddenly you see cougar prints walking in mud. Or you are up on the ridge in late afternoon and you can see the lightning coming. You hurry to get down, the boom boom boom in your ears, the ozone in your nose, and there across the valley God's bow stretches. You cannot help thinking that it would be a good day to die because nothing has ever been so beautiful or so alive and you have never been so pure. You are ready.

The Difference

He consulted with Death about what he should put on his tombstone. Death thought it ought to be something funny. He thought long and hard about it, wrote about it, wrote about it some more, recited it out loud, and thought some more. He wants it to say this: "Every creature alters the world. Irrevocably. No matter how brief, how quiet, how small, there can be no such thing as an inconsequential or obscure life. Everything that becomes lives on forever in the difference it obliges the world to observe. The faintest mark, the subtlest trace, enjoins memory and meaning, for the universe is sentient and its society is pervasive. The message that is each life and each death is thus indelible."

Perfect Silence

In two weeks he ranged from Joshua Tree National Park, where he camped in the perfect silence and fog while something ectoplasmic and sinister circled his tent all night, leaving no footprints, no hoofprints – he ranged from Joshua Tree to the south rim of the Grand Canyon where he stayed up all night on LSD in relentless snow squalls and burned an entire dead pinyon pine to stay toasty discovering that the campfire and the fire in the stars and the fire of the spirit are all the same stuff.

The Dance

Such as the world wherein the dance of the bee is danced on and on so that buzzy others can navigate by the great yellow star to the richest flowers; such as the world wherein the engineering genius of the beaver is implemented with great skill, power and care in the soggy, boggy, foggy woods; such as the world where the strategy that animates the absolute precision of the simultaneous movement of wheeling flocks of birds and schools of fish is successful against predators (look big and confuse with motion); such as the world where it makes perfect sense for the largest creature on the planet, the magnificent blue whale, to sustain itself on krill, one of the smallest creatures on the planet; such as the world where the mysterious blinking yellow lights hovering in the nighttime backyards of the suburban wasteland in summertime are a pretty miracle indeed.

Those Terrorist Flowers

on the air force base
a meadow of cowpen daisies
mowed down

— Jeanne Shannon

Late Summer

by Stuart Bartow

In late summer the soft greens of spring turn richly dark. Along Camden Creek are clusters of wild aster and golden rod, purple and yellow. Surely this is not paradise, but might be a simulacrum of paradise, which raises the question, "Is there fly fishing in heaven?" All fly anglers know the answer to that question. So much so that to ask it is absurd. I sometimes like to think that this world is a rehearsal for the next, that what we experience in this world carries over into the next, and to live joylessly in this world is a squandered life. I find it impossible to believe that you can live a fulfilling life without a strong connection to the natural world. But how do you do that? Possibly paying attention to the details of nature, which fly fishing can make you do. Thoreau on his deathbed when asked about the afterlife, replied, "One world at a time." I, too, have nothing to offer regarding the next world, if one, or many, exist. It could be we simply merge into the universe, or we wake on another shore somewhere, where of course there are fish.

Armed Hiker

Out on the Loyalsock Trail,
in the mountains of northern Pennsylvania,
I'm hiking a few miles
on a perfect, cool fall day.
And while I'm standing on the lip of a waterfall,
just below an amazing stretch
of crumbling sandstone cliffs,
and watching the water splash
over the dark rocks below,
listening to the steady, spattering sound
that makes you feel like you're
a hundred thousand years old,
but in a good way,
someone else hiking alone
is coming up the ravine.
A young guy, in his twenties, I guess.
Lean, muscular. His pack is large,
he's got a red bandana tied around his head,
he's using walking poles, he's moving right along.
But he stops and we say hello.
I wouldn't call him cheerful.
He doesn't smile. He's serious.
"Beautiful day. How far are you going?" I say.
He's doing the whole trail. Fifty-nine miles.
It'll take him till Tuesday.
I notice that his equipment includes
a pistol, strapped to the middle of his chest.
It's in a holster, but it's definitely not concealed. It gleams.

Hmm, what's the proper etiquette? Do I say,
"Nice pistol"? For some reason I don't ask,
and after a couple minutes of wilderness small talk, we say,
"Have a good one," "You too,"
and he heads off again, striding along on his poles.
Now that he's gone, I wish I hadn't
acted as if the gun weren't there.
I wish I'd asked him about it.
There are bears in these mountains,
but I've hiked here forty years,
and only run into one once,
and it took off into the woods.
What was it that he was thinking he might need to shoot?
It might have been an interesting conversation,
in the cool, ancient room of the waterfall.

— Howard Nelson

How I Dream

I dream the way
a tiny green tree frog
with silky-wet fingers
climbs a moist window
in the rainy dark,

a window that reflects
both light and shadow,
joy and sorrow –

an eye without a lid
that looks back at me
when I step closer to see myself,
or all that matters of myself:

a pastel ghost,
and then my brave, true flesh,
roll after roll of hills behind me,
and forests before me,
where everything I do matters,

but leaves no mark
beyond the slim, damp, frog-print
written on fire-forged glass –

glass so clear
it could be water, air,
or life's breath.

— Freya Manfred

Excerpt from *Rice County Odonata Journal: Volume Two*

by Scott King

"To the student of insects high summer is no time for dreaming: it is a time for being afoot and alert."
— Howard Ensign Evans, *The Wasp Farm*

July 25: To St. Olaf. Mostly cloudy, temperature in the low 70s. South of the wooded pond on the grassy margins of the mown trail, male Whitefaced Meadowhawks kept watch from territorial perches, one every ten feet or so. I found a pair mating, in wheel position, the male clasping the female's head, the female curved under to connect with the male – the Odonata are the sole practitioners of this remarkable yin and yang circle while performing sex.

In the reed canary grass around the pond Sedge Sprites and Slender Spreadwings went about their secret lives, almost motionless.

By the time I reached Skoglund Pond, clouds had moved in and I could find no dragonflies. I did kick a few Sedge Sprites and a handful of Hagen's Bluets out of the vegetation near the shore.

I struck out on the prairie meadow trails hoping to see meadowhawks, hoping in particular for Variegated Meadowhawks having recently encountered them in Cottonwood County. The first two meadowhawks were large and solidly red in color. I was unable to net these or any of the subsequent meadowhawks encountered. Mostly I couldn't get close enough to even attempt to net them, so I can't say for certain which species they were.

On the far loop of the prairie, amongst a stand of eight-foot-high cottonwood saplings, I saw a blue darner rise and then land in the meadow not far off the trail. I was able to find it perched, but missed when I tried to net it. Same with the Black-saddlebags cruising above the trail. So it goes.

July 26: To Peat Bog WMA. Being a Sunday afternoon with a few free hours, I visited this nearby wetland. It was sunnier than the last time I stood at the water's edge, and many more dragonflies were on the wing over the water. Again a darner or a Prince Baskettail flew back and forth far out and away from the shore, seldom approaching, and never coming close enough to even entertain the idea of netting it. Eastern Amberwings flew perch to perch much closer to shore, preferring floating mats of algae and protruding sticks. Even once, I was lucky enough to notice, one made a brief touch to a turtle's nose. When one flew by inches away from my feet, I missed yet again. The very first dragonfly I was able to get in the net, was one I had been hoping to see for some time, an Eastern Pondhawk (*Erythemis simplicicollis*). Its eyes and armored nose were bright green, its wide, flat abdomen a fine slaty blue, its terminal appendages white [OC#314319]. Not long afterwards, a few yards down the shore, Blue Dashers (*Pachydiplax longipennis*) sparred with one another, each returning to their respective perches across a small channel… maybe ten feet opposite from the other [OC#314320].

Before leaving, I walked the edges of the gravel road near the WMA parking lot, hoping to kick up a meadowhawk or two from the ditch grass. A local, driving a dusty truck, stopped, rolled down his window, and asked what I was looking for. I told him dragonflies. He said, after a considerable pause, "Are those those things that fly around like helicopters?" "Yep," I replied. "Well, good luck," he said, and drove off. I imagined him shaking his head, having a good laugh around the dinner table that night.

July 29: To Kelly-Dudley Lake. I stood in the lily pads for at least an hour, sticking out like a sore thumb. The dragonflies stayed well away. The fishermen asked questions as they came and went at the landing: "Are you catching frogs?" one couple asked; "What are you looking for out there in the weeds?" another boat full asked. When I informed the latter that I was watching dragonflies, they expressed their best wishes and hoped that I was getting paid at least. I could only shake my head; I doubted I could explain, to them at least, just exactly how I was being paid. My silent reply, kept to myself, was that I'm interning with the dragonflies this summer, hoping to learn from them, to become more familiar with their habitats, their patterns, their ancient skills and abilities, their winged livelihood, their glittering trade. I knew, from recent reading, that the insects evolved on land, that aquatic larvae was a subsequent development. Here I was, land animal up to my knees in water, headed in the same direction. As I stood there, pairs of Calico Pennants (*Celithemis elisa*) tapped the water, touching their eggs to the surface, counting on a few to drift down past the feeding sunfish and survive.

On the lily pads at my knees Skimming Bluets (*Enallagma geminatum*) perched. Like living standards of measure, each was a slender inch including wings, and blue at both ends [OC#314387]. There were flies on the pads as well. Also shiny, pewter-colored beetles

81

with a resemblance, it seemed to me, to the terrestrial tiger beetles. Farther out, over the wide bed of water lilies, pondhawks, dashers, amberwings, and the occasional darner kept my interest.

Seeing a buttonbush tree on the shoreline, I waded over to have a closer look at this unusual tree, which is rather rare in Minnesota. On one of the blossoms, a mud dauber had captured and was stinging a bumble bee. I took a photo of this compact and spherical drama, the kind of incident Jean Henri Fabre would wrote whole books about. My bonus pay for the day.

July 31:   I left at noon for Joe and Nancy Paddock's house in Litchfield. From there we traveled together to Montevideo in western Minnesota for a poetry reading at the Java River coffee shop, where we were joined by poet Athena Kildegaard who had arrived from Morris.

Beforehand, on the way to Litchfield, I stopped at the Henderson public access on the Minnesota River…how could I resist? I collected a Blue-fronted Dancer from near the boat ramp – the only species present, though abundant. For a short while, standing at the river's edge, I attempted to envision the steamboat Frank Steele making its way upstream, its paddle wheel plashing rhythmically through a summer morning, on June 18, 1861. Henry David Thoreau was on board that day as a passenger, taking detailed botanical notes, long lists of scientific plant names, as the boat beat its way up the Minnesota River toward Redwood Agency where he would hear the famed Sioux leader, Little Crow, speak. How difficult to imagine what that day must have been like.

I stopped one more time, nearer to Litchfield, at the public access to Lake Minne-Belle. At this lake there were Stream Bluets and Hagen's Bluets. No dragonflies. At Joe and Nancy's house, we watched a Blue Darner patrolling through their backyard, eating insects above their garden.

Our drive to Montevideo put us on a collision course with an illustrious thunderstorm. It had loomed ahead of us for many miles. Lightning jutted down upon the road just as we turned out of its path. But still it raced beside us on a slant but diminishing tangent, clouds and wind and rain billowed out and overtook us as we made the outskirts of Montivideo. As we parked in town on Main Street the rain came down, a flood washing the chalk-written announcement of our reading from the sandwich board outside the coffee shop. No doubt the storm kept the place from being over crowded. Even still, nearly two dozen people were in the audience, coast and hats dripping around their chairs, as we read our poems. We sold a few books, then ventured down the street to visit with printer Andy Kahmann at his A to Z Letterpress Printing print shop. After a good visit there, after some good laugher at his "Bad Andy" cards, we drove back to Litchfield.

August 1:   Litchfield, Minnesota. I stayed the night with Joe and Nancy Paddock. Their guest room is Joe's attic study, a well-lit, book-lined room with a trap door to prevent guest from falling down the stairs in the middle of the night. I woke early. Not wanting to wake my hosts, I sat and read from Usula Le Guin's *The Waves of the Mind*, enjoying her sardonic, tongue-in-cheek essay that begins "I am a man" but ends with her sly suggestion that it might be a good idea if someone invented old women.

After breakfast, while Joe put the canoe carrier racks on the van, I sat back and relaxed. I talked with Nancy while Joe did all the work. We took the canoe to Dunn Lake for a paddle. Once a lake with clear water, no cabins, and extensive lily beds, it's now developed, ringed by houses, with its water quality degraded by a booming carp population. The carp showed up everywhere along the shore. We heard them slurping the surface. And when not seen or heard their presence could be deduced from the great billowing clouds of sediment and sand in the shallows where they rooted like hogs until disturbed by the passing of the canoe. We found only a tiny remnant of the once extensive lily beds, maybe 50 feet in length and 20 feet in width, where once, according to Joe, who had trapped and fished here in his youth, the lilies had filled the entire bay. Joe also recalled lending a hand in throwing carp out of the stream at the outlet of the lake, when there was still a functioning carp trap. That effort to keep carp out of the lake was given up at some point as resources dwindled. No doubt, in a year or two, the water lilies will be gone; the insects and fish associated with them will, in all likelihood, be gone too. One reason the current survey of Odonata in Minnesota was undertaken was to establish what species are here now so that in the future we will know if changes have occurred. Here, on this small lake, some big changes are in progress, pushing the local Skimming Bluet population out of existence, a shame.

August 5: I drove to Mankato, and spent the afternoon visiting poet John Calvin Rezmerski at his home. We had a grand conversation that covered a whole lot of ground. His role as special agent to the Bill Holm papers, stories of his father and his father's work as operator of a relic steam crane, Charles Hamrum and his work with dragonflies, a new book about carp and the Minnesota River, ghazals, the poetry of Tomas McGrath, Mallard Island, the joys of cooking, chipmunks, Robert Burton's *The Anatomy of Melancholy* are just a few of the topics I can recall.

Driving back, I stopped at the public access on Lily Lake, a small lake just off Highway 60 to the east of the small town of Elysian. Autumn Meadowhawks (*Sympetrum vicinum*) perched in the grass – hundreds of them. They all appeared to be freshly emerged juveniles, no hint yet of the autumnal reds that will replace the tannish oranges and yellows. Probably fifty of these small pale dragonflies lifted from the grass, hovered in synchronistic flight, then returned to their respective perches. Slender Spreadwings and Eastern Forktails put in appearances as well.

On the Lake Following Thunder

there is thunder in a lake

cloud faces,

shadows changing expressions.

the light within the clouds

illuminating like a fluctuating lantern.

world following the seasons joyfully.

the ferry across the ocean of existence.

— Alan Caseline

Swim This Life

Are we not like this,
 slick chill congregants,

orbits wide and expectant,
leftovers from the Eocene.

I've seen how some of us
slip around the ooze

under dim moons,
bodies slab-sided, sometimes glittering.

You are at a great gathering,
but you feel all dried up,

maybe it is time to fit yourself with a wick
and call yourself a hooligan.

And don't I know it,
the ale-wife is always different

than the skip-jack and the hickory.
How many chums have you known

who are partial to wobbling spoons?
No surprise bigmouth buffalo

prefer their doughballs
and nobody cares what bullheads like.

We cluster and feed
on lips of sunrise and storm,

fingerling deep, dream in tangles
of fallen debris, skims of flies

loosening around us,
rainwater raking in noisy fits.

We rudder, hedge and spawn,
married to the force of hunger –

those winglets and odd sparks
that tempt in drift,

leading our desire to possess
until we are pulled up

gasping.

— Diane Jarvenpa

Black Butterflies

(*Vanessa atalanta*)

Their ecstatic storm looms
above the flowers

an entanglement
of glance and eyelash

a stalemate between gravity
and antigravity

the hinges and joints
of an argument

that never stays put
that can't be pinned down.

The black butterflies
pass through the garden

forwarding their loops –
eccentric, haphazard,

admirable, erotic –
straightaway.

— Scott King

90

Lavender Sky

by Helen Ruggieri

The sky is lavender. Violet clouds scud across the top of the gray hills. It's the light though that turns it all miraculous – crystals of ice afloat in the air make a hazy, pale purple scrim over the ordinary world and a full moon emerges from the clouds still red from the sun already fallen over the other side of the mountain.

> what comes, comes
> it's waiting that's hard
> to master

Green Stones

by Casey Brendan*

for many years i would reread the chapters in *rainbow diary*, and enjoy the exciting tales of t. kilgore splake. the main character in splakes's book is a poet, an existential loner like meursault in albert camus's *the stranger*. the poet has chosen to escape the mediocrity of modern civilization by living on an isolated island.

occasionally the poet in splake's *rainbow diary* would take green stones from an ancient mine and trade them for needed things at the "pointe," a small community in malanada. he also used green stones to make jewelry for himself.

now as an aging artist, realizing soon i would be rejoining the earth, i suddenly felt a great force compelling me to find and explore the mystery of the old greenstone mine. after a serious search, i found the poet's exile location. it was a small uninhabited island in northern lake superior. the wilderness growth made my search for the old greenstone mine almost impossible. however, bushwhacking through the dense tangle of deadfall and new forest growth, i finally found the poet's greenstone mining site.

sitting alone in the darkness of the old mine, i felt free from upsetting personal concerns that had distracted my vision of the future. i listened carefully for whispers from the early native miners who used stone tools to extract green stones. i was hoping to learn from their wisdom the secrets of my life and eventually what follows.

dawn's first glow was illuminating the autumn colors at the greenstone mine. on the small lake superior island the blazing foliage was a reminder of the double-rainbow morning in the "cliffs" chapter of splake's *rainbow diary*.

however, the fall season would quickly pass and soon the dry warped leaves would be scattered by the fierce november gales. the endless scraping of black bare branches would create a harsh winter symphony during the bitter arctic of long white.

like splake's *rainbow diary* poet i realized my years had been rapidly vanishing. as a graybeard artist i quickly understood the loss of time and energy to write more poems and make new green rock jewelry. my ancestral bones were made long ago from the material that came swimming across the galaxy from exploded stars. once emerging from the precious earth's womb, all too soon i would have to return to the reality of the earth's hardscrabble soil.

now i seriously wonder if after death a new, deeper reality will exist beyond the continuous worldly hum. splake's *rainbow diary* poet thought about the search for new uncharted lands lying beyond his island home. he also considered leaping off his island's cliffs to fly with the wild birds into another existence.

* Casey Brendan is the pseudonym used by t. kilgore splake in the original publication of this piece.

Susquehannock

Evening stars say
you have made it,
come here foot-sore
with a pack to the hub
of galaxies where
by light the five
rose-breasted grosbeaks
whirled in combative
forest free-for-all,
these eyes stretched
wide as migrants
faded in dusky tangle.
Stars sing welcome
to a mountain where
owl and porcupine
define life's
measure, where man
is but a species,
four miles out
of Conrad, PA
population zero.

— Walt Franklin

Six Reveries on Shells

I.

Before math, mollusks:
blue top and rock whelk,
periwinkle and turban.
Whorl by whorl,
without art or intent,
the gastropods spin their shells
in logarithmic spirals.

II.

Could a wandering heart find home
in a living stone?
To dwell in pearl
and not to know the pattern
of rib or whorl,
the bands of color that spiral
to the shell's tip; to cling,
at low tide, to rock,
shut against air and light.
Could a wandering heart
find solace unseeing?

III.
Pigment and shell, pigment
and shell: this rhythmic
oscillation of secretion:
an interplay of accident
and matter?
Or does the mollusk's mantle,
with each new whorl,
feel its symmetries growing,
know by touch band and stripe,
spoke and spiral, and the colors
that glisten in sun at low tide?

IV.
Scoured clean, a broken curl
of calcium carbonate
bleaches in dry sand.

The sea offers only itself:
a wave's curl,
the foam's sliding lace –

but the absent spiral still spins,
and the heart writes
an algorithm for return.

V.

Shattered, or worn to a single grain,
a stone's heart retreats
again and again
to its new center.
And the snail's shell,
this curl of calcium,
where in its axis
dwells the heart when the mollusk dies?

VI.

Empty, I, too, would wait,
mollusk gone,
for a hermit crab
to dance me across the sand.

— Vicki Graham

Snowstorm after Midnight

The yardlight stares and stares at the storm,
spotlighting every fiber of snow –
like an anonymous monk whose solitude
illuminates the old manuscripts
and long centuries of winter.

Always moving I pause for a moment
and watch the drifting light, each tiny flake
a sled heaped with darkness.

— Scott King

Rural Free Delivery

My heart keeps beating
despite the many reasons
that it might give out—
earthquakes, fires, hurricanes, man's
    inhumanity to man.

Four-thirty AM,
a half hour before sunrise,
the first birds begin
    to sing, telling the dark world:
enter for a chance to win.

Early this morning
by the garden gate I find
a raven's feather
on the lawn, its blue-black vane
    threaded between blades of grass.

Climbing age-twisted
apple trees in the orchard,
I shake their branches
    for whatever I cannot
    reach, combing the grass for falls.

Leaving aside its
   watery phase, a dragonfly
nymph grows transparent
wings and hovers above the same
   pond in which it used to swim.

Folding colored sheets
of paper into the shapes
of tiny boats, I
   set them adrift to carry
my letters to you downstream.

                        — Michael Jewell

Tiger Moths

Tell me, do you ever think of them,
the summer moths whose numbers
no one can count, whose wings
carry hieroglyphs and
tapestries a Persian rug maker
would envy? What astronomer might glean
maps of planets undiscovered
embroidered on their wings? Consider
where they sleep all day while
pretending to be warts or lichen or leaves,
concealed behind shutters, or in the shade
of the eaves. Then to emerge on night's margins,
inside a frequency that belongs only
to them, that we might glimpse,
in our sleep, or between dreams,
legions of them speckling forests, roadsides,
flocking to streetlights and porch lamps,
whirling like Dante's damned, those
lights they mistake for stars,
those beings we mistake for moths.

— Stuart Bartow

Everything I Needed to Know about the Truth, I Learned from a Tree

by Benjamin Green

curling inland
thick gray fog mists the needles
on the redwood boughs

Sometimes the lens that is Trinidad Head bends the light into a mountain standing over the sea. Sometimes it bends the light to make a small lichen covered rock. Today, the light lifts one tree, stands it up against the sky as a blackened silhouette, and reveals the shape of the wind's smile. Today, it is an alder beside the trail, a not quite straight line of blurred white light complete with the blue sweep of a jay.

I woke up this morning in a contemplative mood. I began the day wanting to think about "truth." Wallace Stevens wrote, "Perhaps the truth depends upon a walk around the lake." I have Trinidad Head, so

103

off I went, and now stand contemplating the story revealed in the shape of this alder.

Sometimes science helps to make sense of things without taking away the mystery inherent in them. I will never know what it is like to be a tree, but at least I can know what a tree is. A tree is a woody perennial plant having single main stem that raises itself above the ground to gain sunlight. The tree has to be able to support itself, especially in the wind, thus the specialized stem we know as a trunk. Unfortunately, science has little to offer me when it comes to the concept of "the truth."

The summer after Karen Fisher was murdered, I left Humboldt County. I moved to Fort Bragg, on the Mendocino coast to the south. For five years I helped my family run a business in town. When a fire destroyed our store, I decided it was time to return to college. I wanted to be a writer and I thought there were some things I needed to know.

Philosophy was part of my self-designed major at Humboldt State University. In one class a professor lectured for the entire quarter only about the philosophical bases behind the term "behavior." We spent ten weeks reading and talking (or more accurately: listening to the professor talk) about what an "action" was. I came to the conclusion that most academic philosophy was just words about words. All the talk about "action" was just that: talk.

I took a class on the philosophy of the truth from the same professor. This course was remarkably similar to the one concerning "actions." The man lectured, arguing with the thoughts of others in our texts, trying to come to terms with what constituted the truth. I decided that all the talk about truth was just that: more talk.

What do we talk about when we talk about truth? What do we mean when we say something is true? Is the truth a substance, a quality, a process, or a relationship? Is it merely a property of an expression or a declaration of what is really there? Is the truth a search or a conversation? There are a lot of ideas. There are dictionary answers, psychological answers, phenomenological answers, experiential answers.

I live in a palpable world, where boot heel strikes the earth, where toes stretch in beach sand, where the sun warms me and the wind chills my body. When I talk about the truth, I want to talk about my *sense* of it and not about my *ideas* of it. Facts (another word often used interchangeably with "truth") are not linguistic entities. Facts are an "objective state of affairs." They are specific, detailed, and testable, and must be locatable in the natural order, not just in the human intellect. Evidence is truth; the truth can be observed and measured. The truth happens outside of the mind, although we abstract it into a concept inside our mind. It can be validated, corroborated, verified.

The truth is making reality work for us; the truth is how we "handle" reality.

We do not determine the veracity of a factual claim by reasoning; we use our senses to decide whether we accept a factual statement. The truth is registered emotionally; we feel it. The truth is also felt physically, best exemplified by the human body's reaction as measured on a lie detector. We have specific physiological reactions when we know, or even just suspect, that we are lying or have been lied to. We have different physiological reactions when we think we are telling or hearing the truth. Our figures of speech reveal this physiological relationship: "I know it in my heart," "I trust my gut reaction," "in my head…"

The systematic, academic, school-room philosophic study of "the truth" usually breaks into two schools: the correspondence theory of truth and the coherence school of truth. Plato usually gets credit for first stating the ideas of the correspondence school. He gets credit for a lot in the field of philosophy, and it is sometimes hard to remember that there were thinkers, even in Greece, before him. The Pre-Socratic Greeks were perhaps the first to realize that the results of the logic of linguistics severed the truth from experience, maybe even severed the truth from speech. They saw how the connection between language and truth was dissolved with logical analysis.

Socrates lived from about 475 BCE to 405 BCE; Plato lived from about 425 BCE to 355 BCE. Some of the earliest Greek thinkers date back to 625 BCE. Thales was one of the first recorded. He is credited with being the first to seek the reality behind phenomena, referred to by these ancient Greeks as "the immortal principle." "Water is the substrate from which all things are derived." Anaximenes, born around 566 BCE, wrote that "everything is a dilation or compression of a single substance: air." Diogenes, a contemporary of Socrates agreed: air explained all phenomena: "Air is life and intelligence, it is everything. Air is God." Heraklitus, born in 540 BCE, found fire, or "monistic flux," to be the unity behind seeming discrepant existence. Xenophanes, perhaps dating back to 580 BCE, grounded reality in earth; "Everything comes from the soil and returns to the soil."

The original elements of water, air, fire, and earth sufficed as explanations for these Pre-Socratics. Truth was somehow located in one or more of these immortal principles. Anaximander, a contemporary of Thales, introduced abstraction; "The originative substance is the Indefinite, the non-limited." Empedocles, born around 500 BCE, contributed emotion to the mixture: "Love and hate rule the cosmos through their purposeless dialectic of comings together and rendings assunder." Anaxagoras, from the same time period, ushered in consciousness: "The mind creates and rules the universe." Parmenides argued for logic: "Being is bound by logic. Whatever exists must be thinkable and logical." Zeno used the arguments of logic to prove that logical arguments were absurd when applied to human experience. Protagoras, also from the same time, announced humanism: "Man is the measure of all things."

Some of the Pre-Socratics grew confused by all the arguing. Metrodorus blurted out: "I deny that we know whether we know anything or nothing. I deny that we know even whether knowing or not knowing exists, nor in general whether anything exists or not. Everything exists which anyone thinks." Cratylus gave up. He decided that it was not possible to say anything true about anything, so he abandoned speech altogether and communicated only by gesture. Silence, it seems to me, is the honorable path in such a situation.

The correspondence theory of truth holds that there is only one reality, one world, and that there is only one true description of that reality. Naming is the simplest form of language that matches reality. Description is the only form of truth possible. The truth is when our words accurately depict the world, or if there is an agreement between a statement and the facts of reality. At its best, this school shows how language and reality interpenetrate. At its worst, human conceptions are totally divorced from the natural world.

The correspondence school can get reduced to the point where the truth can be expressed only as one type of sentence: the proposition, the "if/then." Sometimes, known as the atomic school, it is thought that if discrete atoms make up matter, then the truth must consist of discrete independently verifiable propositions.

Others argue that the world can be described correctly with *various* incompatible terms. Truth (or "proof" – the words are sometimes used synonymously) is the outcome of a rational inquiry that is internalized individually. Our personal understanding of a sentence, of a description, is what constitutes the truth, and there can be as many valid understandings as there are persons.

What is shared in common in the correspondence school is the relationship between language and the truth. Saying is equated with verification. Only statements can be true, or false; truth is the outcome of the words used in making statements. In the correspondence school, when the issue is truth, humans cease to have a direct relationship with reality; it is our words that have interesting, detailed connections with the world. Words communicate the world; if they are descriptive or demonstrative, then they are true. Language is proof of the world. Access to the truth ends in the mind; it resides in our thoughts about things.

The coherence school of truth resides solely in words, also. No longer does a statement have to agree with nature; within this school one statement only has to agree with other statements to form a system of thought. Something is true if it is part of a series of truths. The truth fits together, it coheres, with other truths. Our perception is limited by our language, by the practices of articulation. Access to reality is impossible, access to objectivity is impossible; language is reality. We can give up the search for truth as a frustrated impossibility, or we can face the limits, "out face" our doubt, and try to find our truth within language. We can try to make a life for ourselves within language.

Others reject both schools and toss the whole argument in the garbage. "Truth," they say, is a meaningless term. We could say what we mean without using the terms "true" or "truth." Usually, they argue, the whole discussion is only about words. We are not even talking about Truth, but about what makes a statement true, and in that case truth is totally dependent upon what criteria for validity are chosen in advance. Sure, language is an attempt to refer to things, but reference is not the truth in language: a statement is true if it obeys the rules of usage within the language.

One definition of truth I remember was: "Statements that agree with convention, that we are conditioned to speak." Another one I remember paraphrased truth as "I am right." The best definition, for me, was: "It's true if it's true." Many who are dismissive of the entire conversation regarding truth come to the same conclusion: the truth is experienced easily, seen simply, is a basic human notion – but it is

110

not definable, or cannot be said without great difficulty, cannot be explained to someone who does not share the same viewpoint.

The thinker who impressed me most when it came to the subject of truth was Martin Heidegger. He said that the truth was a process and a relationship. He knew that the truth could not be systematized without losing it. He knew that the truth was a concept wrapped up in not just language and the senses, but in our relationships as well. For Heidegger, when anything arcs into one's perception, the observed and the observer are together in a membership that implies a relationship.

Heidegger wrote that rationality and the practice of logic were self-limiting contrivances that trivialized the idea of the truth. The truth was part of living a thoughtful life. Like the Tao, the truth was a "way." Heidegger's way is best characterized by "seeking." The measure of a man is what he seeks. Part of seeking, is to be open, to be willing to be moved. The truth is when something is brought into view; the thing is moved so we can see it or we move so we can see it. One of the things I liked about Heidegger was that he showed how complex, abstract concepts could often be understood quite simply in everyday language. The "naked truth" is a phrase that describes how the truth is a revelation, an unconcealment, a disrobing. The truth is brought into view. The truth is when we can see clearly. The truth is an appearance, and Heidegger knew that if we deprived the truth of appearance, it lost the best part of its reality: appearance is a sensual relationship. Because the truth was a visual sensation, Heidegger related the truth to the physical senses. The truth makes us feel something in our body; it is not merely intellectual or mental

Heidegger's viewpoint applied to language, also. As in the correspondence school, Truth was equated with the correctness of an assertion. For Heidegger, however, assertions were "representations," and representation, too, was a relationship.

Heidegger also warned that the truth, what was in sight, the "what is seen," is not always a positive thing. Negativity exists. It is a harsh world, out there. "That's what you get for looking."

So, that is what I get for thinking about the truth: an image of a frustrated look on a professor's face and a reminder that it is a harsh world out there. The trees on Trinidad Head tell me much the same. While the requirements for trees are abundant on Trinidad Head – water, sun, and air – the actual real life trees on Trinidad Head are mostly stunted: wind-beaten, rain-drowned, salt-poisoned, sun-deprived. They grow, but not much or well, and I doubt if they grow old.

It is late March, and most of the native deciduous trees – the alders, elderberry, cascara – have already leafed. In the breeze today, the leaves are busy, in earnest. The cottonwood I planted in my yard to honor one of my publishers is waiting for a few more days of warmth. Almost every leafy plant has renewed itself, except the maple. The maple – what is keeping the maple? Songbirds call for the foxglove to rise, to dance and bloom. It is spring and there is a smell of growth. I guess it must be the odor of chlorophyll asserting itself like the rank of skunks dead on the side of the freeway.

Right now, I am captivated by an alder. Windblown, lopsided, with many dead branches, it is still a tree and despite all the challenges it faced, and faces, it never stopped growing. The wind rips at the white bark, shredding and scarring; it tears at the leaves, breaks twigs, twists limbs and branches. The tree leans, bends, but it is still a tree, and every twist and bend and bump in the skeletal shape is a story.

I pick off a leaf. This one is green, of course, somewhere between permanent light green and sap green on my watercolor palette. The palm-sized leaf flares from the stem like a bowl with near perfect symmetry; it gradually tapers to a right-angled tip. Each leaf has a central vein of lighter green that reaches straight toward the tip. Fainter diagonal veins angle off at 45 degrees every quarter inch or so; these diagonals join together in right-angled pairs at the center vein. The leaf edge is serrated and jagged – with the leaf tips at the end of each diagonal vein line. The leaves *look* perfectly symmetrical, but if I fold one in half, the two halves do not match.

The underside of the leaf is lighter green than the outer, but the veins are more distinct when viewed from below because on the bottom side of the leaf the veins are raised rather than etched. When I look closely, I can see the many micro-veins that come off the diagonals. All these little veins join together to transform the leaf into a jigsaw puzzle.

The top of each leaf is dark and shiny. The leaf bottoms are rough on the fingers; the tops are smooth and smell like a green gas. (When a person takes a breath in a forest, hundreds of chemicals expired by trees enter the nose and go straight to the brain; they enter the lungs and blood and affect how we feel). It is only March, and even though the leaves are brand new, most of them are already wind-torn and insect-chewed. It *is* a tough world out there.

Alders keep their leaves well into winter here on the coast. Some years it seems like the new leaves push the old ones off the trees. A few weeks ago, when the tree was leafless, the trunk looked whiter than it does now, and for those few weeks when the tree was leafless, just trunk and branches, I could trace the growth that made the tree's shape. This tree that has captured my attention grew straight up during its youth, it branched rarely, the growth was up – and, if I could see, down into the roots – where it did the most good. Then, it took a radical turn when its trunk top broke off; the branch that became its leading tip (and new trunk) leaned the tree toward the sunlight. Just a week ago, this tree held long tendrils, the alder's flower, that grew rapidly downward. Then, small, leathery and wrinkled leaves appeared, and quickly unfurled to a smooth, shiny palm-sized leaf like the one I now hold in my hand.

In the summer, the leaves will begin to fall, mostly blown off by the wind. Insects will mar the near-perfect symmetry even more. Green cones will turn dark brown. In the fall, the leaves will begin to turn yellow and then brown. The wind and the rain will bring most of them down, but a few will linger until late winter. The whole cycle repeats every year with a few variations as the weather dictates.

The alder is not typical of deciduous broad-leaved trees. Rather than spreading as it grows, most alders grow in thickets. They are one of the first trees to cover a clear cut or fire damaged forest. The clump of trees maximizes leaf surface to capture sunlight and shade out competition. Alders also often sprout under a conifer canopy. In this case, the tree grows up and toward any available sunlight. Likewise, branches are not used for spreading but for finding sunlight. The alder in front of me sprouted in the thick brush of Trinidad Head. It grew straight up to gain the sunlight, spread some branches to capture more light, and then its tip broke off so one of the branches became the new tip and the new trunk.

Further up the trail is an example of a conifer: a Sitka spruce. Unlike most broad-leafed trees, (and like the alder), the spruce's growth is upward. Although it grows tall and straight, the Sitka spruce is not the most beautiful of trees. Trinidad is just about the southernmost point in their range, so maybe the specimens here are not prime examples. They always look "unkempt" and messy to me. Although they have some large sweeping branches, smaller, thin bushy branches climb the entire tree as well. The branches descend, the twigs trail, and the needles are stiff. Many branches support a thick beard of lichen. The lower branches are often shaded out by the density of the growth above, so the lower trunks are studded with dead stubs.

A forest of Sitka spruce is a sunless place; the density of the canopy allows little sunlight and there is almost no undergrowth, just mossy piles of fallen branches. The tree buttresses itself with a wide base and the roots spread at ground level. It is spring, so this tree is covered with light green needle buds. The ground is littered with the cones. These cones are small, about three inches long, but they are wet and heavy, and in windstorms they batter my metal roof at home. The bark of a Sitka spruce is purplish and pink brown with gray and green stains from moss and lichen. The bark is cracked, flaky, and scaled; it peels from the bottom. The wood of a Sitka is fibrous and stringy, very hard to split, and full of sticky sap. I have heard it is used to make beautiful guitar sound-boards.

This tree, like most pines, is a *gymnosperm*: it started out as a "naked" seed, or a seed that is not enclosed in an ovary. (Tree evolution is believed to have gone something like this: ferns were first. They are soft-fibered plants that reproduce via spores. Ferns unwind their coiled fronds like a snake. They reproduce with spores: the spores drop on the ground and grow into a flat plant that has sex organs. These plants then produce a seed. Gymnosperms came next. They developed the first seeds and the woody stem. *Angiosperms* came last: they are the flowering trees, like fruits and nuts. While we think of evolution as a phenomenon that works at a nearly geological pace, the plant ecosystems most of us are familiar with are very recent. The Douglas fir forest is only 11,000 years old. The coastal redwood ecosystem has only been in existence for 9,000 years. Some existing redwoods are believed to be near 2,000 years old. This means they may be only the third or fourth generation of their species.) For some conifers, like the fir, it takes seventeen months for pollen and egg to produce a seed. Most conifers produce a lot of seeds, but they are incredibly small. 6,000 redwood seeds weigh less than one ounce. Redwoods produce tons of seeds for each seedling that reaches 10 feet tall. Less than one-tenth of one percent of seeds become trees.

The Sitka spruce, on the other hand, produces few seeds, even though they weigh only 1/13,000 of an ounce. One tree might produce only 100 seeds per year.

One of those seeds might germinate; most germinated seeds are then destroyed by fungi. Sitka spruce can live for 800 years and grow up to 300 feet tall; a long-lived tree might produce ten surviving offspring.

Here on the coast, despite their tolerance for salt spray, the trees live for only fifty to a hundred years and grow to maybe 150 feet. Because they lack a taproot, they often blow down in the wind, and because they grow together in monotonous groves, they often blow down in clumps. Wind is second only to fire as the cause of forest destruction.

This Sitka spruce started as a seed. It was lucky enough to germinate. It may have lain dormant through a winter. Next, was to root itself. Most trees grow their root first. And like most trees, the Sitka spruce does not have a taproot; the roots spread rather than go down. A cap drills down, cells divide and differentiate. Some cells begin to transfer water upwards. How they do this is still a mystery, but a redwood tree can lift water more than 400 feet over 36 hours. Nutrients from the seed travel down to the roots and then back up as water movement begins. Some cells become auxins, or plant growth hormones. The root will bond with fungi. This allows for greater contact with the soil, water and nutrients (which benefits the tree); the fungus gains access to the tree's sugar stores. The stored sugar is used to synthesize *macromolecules*, or the building blocks of the physical tree. Trees contain two types of fiber: cellulose and lignin. Cellulose is strong, but it is brittle. Lignin is also firm, strong, tough and woody, but it allows the tree some flex in the wind.

The tree starts on the stem next. What defines a tree as a tree is the single giant stem, or trunk. At first, the tree relies on stored starch. When that is gone, the tree must grow needles to photosynthesize food. The stem pushes up the seedcase, two seed leaves sprout; then, the stem becomes a developing shoot with true leaves. We have a tree. For broad-leaved trees, the growth is usually up and out. For conifers, the growth is up. A Sitka spruce may grow two inches in its first year. As long as the temperature stays above 38°F, the tree will grow continuously.

Of course, the spruce does not have typical leaves. Conifers have a specialized leaf known as a needle. For a tree that grows up rather than out, the needle maximizes leaf surface. A 200 foot tall Douglas fir has nearly three acres of leaf surface. Most conifers have about ten times the leaf surface of a similarly sized deciduous broadleaf tree. Needles also have the advantage that they can last for more than one season. Most conifers have needles that remain on the tree for two to three years. The bristlecone pine retains its needles for up to fifty years (the average for a bristlecone is seventeen years). The needles start as soft buds. Every spring there is some new growth at the end of the branches. My mother used to say these buds were "soft as a baby's butt." But they all face the same wind and eventually grow hard. One of the ways you can recognize a Sitka spruce as a Sitka spruce is that the needles "stick you."

There are three types of trees: broad-leaved, conifer, and palm. They all "work" the same way: a trunk filled with sap transports nutrients down from the leaves and transports water and minerals up from the ground. The bark of a tree is partly dead, partly alive; its purpose is to protect the tree from fire and insects. Leave start as buds. Some buds contain the leaf growth for an entire season; some are just "starters." Leaves take sunlight, water, and carbon dioxide to make sugar. The sugar is used as the fuel to make cellulose and lignin, the tissue of the tree. A simple leaf is a single leaf that comes from one bud; compound leaves refer to the many leaflets that emerge from a single bud. Needles and scales are specialized types of leaves. Trees also have flowers. Most trees are wind-pollinated, but fruit and nut trees have insect-pollinated flowers (sometimes birds and bats help out too).

What does all this talk of trees have to do with the "truth?" More than you might think, for the word *truth* has its roots (pun intended) in the word *tree*. Trace the words backwards and you come to the middle English *trewe* (for true) and *tree* (for tree). Old English gave us *treowe* (for true or faithful) and *treow* (for tree). These, in turn, had old high Germanic and Indo-European roots. "Faithful" in the old high Germanic was *gitruiuwi*; in Sanskrit the roots were *daruna* (hard) and *daru* (wood) and *deru* (solid) and *dru* (for tree) (Put "dru" together with "wit" or "wid" ((meaning "to know")) and you get druid: *knower of the tree*). Old Norse added *tre* (for tree) and Greek contributed *drys* (for wood).

Our figures of speech reveal the depth of the relationship between the words. Think of "truth trees" used in logic. Think of the "tree of knowledge" present in almost every culture. One theory holds that the truth is only accessible through a mediator, or oracle; the first oracles were trees, the word "oracle" comes from the same root as the word "oak."

Humans and trees evolved together. The redwood forest ecosystem that is only 9,000 years old, the Douglas fir forest ecosystem that is only 11,000 years old, have both been home to humans for that entire span.

Trees figure strongly in human mythology. They are sacred symbols in ritual and folklore. Trees resemble the best of what humans aspire toward in terms of personality, traits, and experience. Stand tall, be strong, sink your roots.... They are regarded as intelligent and full of knowledge: their deep roots absorb the wisdom of the past, but they can also see into the future. They seem permanent, have longevity, but are changeable and beautiful. Trees have souls and spirits. They were good friends. If you had a favor to ask, you asked a tree, tracking its bark with your fingers or hand. When the favor was granted, you returned to the tree and rapped your knuckles on the tree as a token of thanks. Ever hear the phrase "knock on wood"?

So it is not too strange to discover that trees were one of the first objects to be worshipped as sacred beings or deities. The first ideal was a tree. Trees were symbols of *life*. Nearly every culture in the east and west has a tree of life. The tree varies; it might be the oak, the ash, the palm, the cedar, the sycamore, the cassia or the bo. Many cultures also have a tree of knowledge, a symbol of the awakening of the moral sense in humanity, the origin of the concepts of good and evil, of right and wrong, of mortality and immortality. Some believe that trees gave birth to humans (which gives new meaning to "family tree"). Some thought humans were transformed into trees at death. Some peoples believed in a "guardian tree."

This concept of the tree as the cradle of being was probably best demonstrated by the Norse and their belief in *Yggdrasill*, an ash that towered over the universe. The tree had three roots: the past, the present, and the future. It had three branches: the center one supported the Earth, the others bound the universe together. The tree's leaves were clouds. The tree's flowers and fruits were stars.

Trees are also symbols for renewal and mystery. Much about a tree is unknown and hidden. Stuff hides in the shadows, things hide behind the leaves, under the bark, under the ground, and in the roots. They rustle and whisper secrets; they sigh and lure one toward mystery.

The list of trees and what they symbolize is long: redwoods are the spirits of great warriors; the plane represents genius; the yew means death, grief, sorrow, faith and resurrection; the myrtle stands for marriage; the willow personifies forsaken love; the walnut is a sign for bad luck; the sycamore indicates mirth; the pine stands for friendship; the palm represents triumph; the hazelnut symbolizes commerce; the olive is a well known symbol for peace. These are just a few, and the meanings the same tree stands for may vary from culture to culture.

In that college class years ago, following the thoughts of the great thinkers as they pondered the truth was like following a leaf or some pollen or a seed as it drifted on the wind. I might as well have wished it were as simple to follow or trace the truth as it is the path from tree root to trunk to branch to leaf-tip, or that I could measure the progression of ideas as easily as I could the growth rings of a tree. But I could not, and still cannot. The truth *is* like a tree: study a tree – you cannot see all sides of it at once, you cannot see all the parts at once; focus on only one part or side and you will lose all the other parts or sides. Human understanding of the world is like a tree sprouting from the granite fist of solid rock: the roots feel along the face of the world like a blind person, find a crevice, a cranny, and force their way in, expand, take hold, strengthen, then run in a crooked line, following the path of least resistance.

But in the end, I must say, everything I needed to know about the truth, I learned from a tree. What I have learned about living a thoughtful life, about seeking, could have been taught by a tree: Remember that you are never by yourself, but if you choose to see yourself as isolate and alone and solitary, then you had better grow up straight and strong and well-balanced. Stand still and tall; be quiet; perhaps you will hear a singing bird. Aim high, touch the sky, point upwards to the things you cannot reach, look forward, but shelter and shade those things beneath you. Grip the ground, root fast and first in the earth, spread your arms and be the voice of the wind. Bear the weight of heaven and cloud. It is okay to shake like a leaf, and it is definitely okay to turn over a new leaf now and then. Do not be afraid to go out on a limb. Think timeless thoughts. Be persistent and patient. Adapt to change when it comes. Hold the world together, and be filled with light.

Just like beauty, I think the truth was there before eyes could see it or brains could fashion the concept of it or mouths could tongue the sound of it into a word, and some of it, hopefully, we will leave alone enough to survive after us. And if you are confused, stand before your confusion like a tree. Stand still. Trees are not lost. Let the truth find you. And I would like to believe, that when it comes into view you will know it and you will know why you came. *You come too.* You are welcome here.

Sunset on the Shore of No Man's Land

A black protuberance of rock
suffers an encroachment of tide.

Eroding, out-of-balance cliffs
losing their definition.

Lingering sunlight redefines
indistinct shapes even as they

merge, as they become one.

— Alan Catlin

The Star on The Hunter's Shoulder

Last night we gazed at Orion.

An astronomer told us
that Betelgeuse may burst
into a supernova
tonight
next week
a thousand years from now.

Or that already
it may have done so.

And who can tell
when the light
will reach us?

— Jeanne Shannon

Tamed by the Gentle Alone

Scattered laid-out as they fell
limbs, large, color-faded
broken from central trunks
reconsidered, cracked length,
bark long peeled
sap dried like glue.
There were other branches,
others quicker to the sun,
wind, piled snow, freeze & thaw
the weight, the lost subtlety
as much as anything
caused their fall.

Next to them lies smaller debris.
left when a strong gust
beheaded their purpose
fresh pine branches
litter the ground
life and growth still close,
green needles intact
sap running from ripped
connection and tumble bruises
sap like slow blood
run out to freeze
in the morning cold

The wind restrains the clouds
cannot hold back the weather
cannot bind the seasons
cannot shape the forest
small ways, gentle expression.
one tree, one branch

When you reach out
for what others see
any new refinement
of your essence
holds the promise
of a more lasting touch

— Alan Caseline

A Camping Trip
Is Like a Shooting Star

Slaloming Route 28
in the Adirondack Park
in the canoe-carrying car
solitary after separating
from daughter and grandsons
at Blue Mountain Lake
where they went south
and I went west
after camping four days
on Little Tupper Lake –
little only because
smaller than Tupper,
Little Tupper five miles long,
not a little lake at all,
and known for its winds.

We paddled in
to campsite 3, on its own island.
That was something,
having your own island,
how often does that happen in life?
I'd camped there before, hoped it would be open,
and there it was, no canoe pulled up,
no one there, a vacancy among the trees.
Spacious enough, fire pit, good spot for tent.
Other amenities: Good branch for bear rope –

though bear swimming out to the island, not very likely.
Bathroom facilities – box with a lid –
a little way off from campsite.
Going there to check it out, a snake in the path.
Not big, not an anaconda;
harmless, not a rattler.
Just a garter, maybe two feet long.
A healthy looking snake, gleaming black,
and a snake in the path
is always unexpected, is always something.
The boys came running,
but before they could catch it
it quickened and slithered
and disappeared into the rocks under the bushes.
And we wondered, what's the snake population
on a small island – and how did they get out here anyway?
Why did they cross a quarter of a mile of water?
So many mysteries.

On one end of the island, sheer rocks, fifteen feet high.
To call them cliffs
wouldn't be lying.
Excellent for jumping off
with grandsons, they old enough, 9 and 12,
me just young enough, 69,
to partake in such sport.
Water at the foot plenty deep,
fifteen or twenty feet.
I couldn't touch bottom, or rather, didn't want to –
it was dark and cold down there.
Climb up rocks, pause, look around, consider.

Then, leap, plummet through thin air,
plunge.
Come up, swim over to rocks, climb up,
do it again, sometimes singly, sometimes together.
We have invented a new Olympic event:
synchronized cliff jumping.
Stand lined up on cliff edge, poised –
1…2…3… Jump!
Everyone doing a cannonball!
Jumping off cliffs is something.
And swimming around
in deep cool water beneath them.

Back at campsite, pretty soon,
the first pair of loons,
coming in close to the island, quietly cruising.
One always hopes they will be here.
Wonderful the way they dip under.
Guess where they will come up,
and never be exactly right.

Next day, set out to paddle
to the far end of the lake,
then go up the winding stream,
with occasional beaver dams
to lift the canoe over.
Have lunch at Rock Pond.
There are some nice lunch rocks there.
But the wind was blowing pretty strong
out on the lake that day, coming right at us,
slow progress, hard going –
so instead we stopped on the sandy beaches

along the north shore,
took long walks along them,
seeing what there was to see.
First in the distance, then, gradually, close up.
Ambling along, walking on sand, sometimes sloshing.
Stopping now and then to swim,
whenever we want to.
Walking along long wilderness beaches is something.
Maybe the weather reports predicting rain
kept people home – for whatever reason,
very few people on the lake,
only three or four canoes or kayaks
passed by the whole day.
Never made it to Rock Pond. Maybe next year.

The next day we crossed the lake
and explored the south shore.
And as we paddled, a bald eagle
came in from behind us, coasting low above us.
"Look – a bald eagle!"
It glided in and landed up ahead of us
in a wind-swept pine
that leaned out over the lake.
A high branch, but close to earth
by eagle standards.
We paddled slow and quiet,
soon could see it clearly,
a clear long moment
of eagle, until it decided
it didn't want this much attention,
hunched its shoulders,
leaned forward, as if it would fall of the branch,

but not falling, instead opening
its wings in take-off nonchalant and powerful
and flapped away over the water
toward parts unknown.
It was really something.

Climbing out of the tent in the morning,
seeing on the tip of the island my daughter
doing her yoga, doing sun salutes,
not just a name, the sun actually rising
above the misty lake stretched out in front of her.

Changeable weather in Adirondack lakes.
The way the wind stirs.
The way you see it coming.
We'd stopped on a rocky island,
big enough to grow a few bushes, but just barely.
Too small to have a name on the map.
We checked it out. We walked around it.
Took a swim off the sloping boulder side.
But all the while we could see
a darkened bank of clouds
gathering at the end of the lake.
And then the rain started, first over there,
then coming toward us,
the riled-up surface moving closer.
It took only a couple minutes
for the stampeding rain to reach us.
At first we thought it was hail, it hit us so hard.
We stood in the downpour.
It was wild – to say it was thrilling

wouldn't be lying.
Standing on treeless rocky island
in bathing suits,
millions of raindrops
tearing up the lake, pounding down on us.
The boys started yelling,
not in fear, but joy,
of something so wet
and pounding happening –
standing out in the teeming rain on a rock in a big lake.
It was something.
Luckily, no lightning.

It rained a couple of other times during our stay.
It rained in the night as we lay
in the tent. It was still raining
in the morning.
We put on ponchos
and put in some time, slow time,
standing around among the dripping trees.
In another way, that was something too.

Days it didn't rain, after supper we paddled
to the beaver bog, half a mile from our campsite,
and in the meandering channel
we practiced the lesson
of being quiet.
The boys got it.
Coming around a curve,
dark shapes moving
in the water ahead

before the whap and splash
which is always a dusky something.

What am I forgetting?
Oh, meals – cooked on Coleman stove,
food from small packages poured into boiling water.
Soup, macaroni, never so delicious,
flavored, as they say, with fresh air and hunger.
Some string beans brought from the garden.
Heating up water for tea in plastic cups –
civilized cups of wilderness tea – so relaxing,
sitting on a log, or canvass folding chair, by the fire.
For breakfast, pancakes flipped carefully
by boy with spatula,
with 100% pure maple syrup.

When it's dark, before going into the tent,
before rustling into sleeping bags,
sitting on rocky shore,
gazing at sky and seeing a shooting star.
A camping trip is like a shooting star.

And then night, four of us in tent.
Playing cards by flashlight.
Then, complete darkness, lying there waiting
for sleep to come.
And the loons
did not let us down.
Out of the night, out of some corner
of the big cornerless lake,
came their looning,

which is something, if anything is something.
The boys hadn't heard it before, but now they have.

Then the silence itself, still lake night.
Just a few campsites here and there, canoes pulled up.
The great silence –
that was really something.

— Howard Nelson

Wild Grasses

by Helen Ruggieri

In late June wild grasses bloom, heavy multicolored seed heads in dark red, shades of purple. I used to love to walk through the fields then picking bunches of purple tipped grass surrounded with delicate airy heads of redtop. The Japanese author of *The Tale of Genji* is Murasaki Shikibu, and Murasaki can be translated as purple grass or purple clover.

> purple headed grasses
> at the bottom of the field
> ensnaring twilight

There are 1000's of kinds of grasses – some so similar you need a microscope to examine the seed heads. Timothy, orchard grass, reed, canary grass, bromegrass, fescue – planted for dairy herds, because they do well in the acid soil of this valley. Their seed has flown on the wind.

I'd sell dried grasses, bunches of wild flowers, at street fairs and fests to people who didn't know the names but recognized the beautiful colors, the shapes of what most dismissed as "weeds."

Native grasses don't even have common names. When I was little I used to look into the grass as if it were another world – from afar the grass looked like one stretch of flat green, but closer – small ground clover vines, eyebright, crab grass, plantain, dandelion, birdfood grass. How complicated everything is I'd think. I tried to paint a picture using all the various colors of green the paint box allowed. Looking at my close-up blobs of various greens the teacher suggested I try something else. Then, I didn't have the words to tell her what it was. And so, like a hunter-gatherer I stalked words, the names of things.

How to Imitate a Birch Tree

The weeping willows
get it wrong.
Stand up straight,
your back will thank you.

Even rooted,
you, too, can dance
in certain weathers.

Receive
both butterflies and moths,
though it's tempting
to discriminate
in beauty's favor.

After devastating fire,
be first to arise.

Stand together against
the oppressions of winter.

When your static life
begins to bore you, imagine
you might be buoyant
as a canoe.

Meanwhile, allow yourself
a modest shine.

— Susan Cohen

On the River

When you fish Crusher Pool
Use a 6 wt rod,
Throw a good-sized streamer.

Far across the Kennebec,
You'll hear screeching;
An eagle
In the tallest white pine.

Double-haul a long cast,
Strip the fly in
Fast against the current.

Then you'll hook
A big smallmouth
In the back eddy.

Watch it
After you bend
To the water and
Release the fish.

Once,
As I stood back up,
Talons grazed my hair.

— Gene Grabiner

Woods Wandering

by Walt McLaughlin

I stepped off the logging road, pushing through a tangle of young spruce blocking the way, and felt my nerves loosen for the first time in months. Springtime verdure was abundant in the lowlands, but in the mountains the leaf buds of the trees were just opening. The chill of winter held fast to the shadowy corners of the forest where patches of dirty snow lingered. I forged ahead, tracing a tiny stream back to its source, guessing that it led to the small, unnamed pond indicated on my topographical map. I was out for three days in a largely overlooked corner of Groton State Forest in eastern Vermont, with a few essentials stuffed into a small rucksack on my back – just the wild and me. It was almost as good as being back in the Alaskan bush.

The sun broke through the clouds overhead. I broke a sweat, even though I was going only a mile an hour. I stripped off a sweater, stuffed the black bush hat I'd been wearing into my pack, then knelt next to the stream long enough to splash a little water into my face. I let my beard drip dry as I continued uphill, going deeper into the woods. A woodpecker cried in the distance then all was quiet. The ground leveled out. The murmur of the tiny stream faded as it fractured into countless seeps emerging from moss-covered rocks. I crossed the muddy remnant of a snowmobile trail and soon spotted a patch of water glistening through a break in the forest. I had reached the pond.

I followed a set of moose tracks halfway around the pond then stopped to remove my pack. I crouched behind a large rock, scanning the surface of the clear, shallow water for signs of trout activity. I saw one rise then another as I extended a collapsible fishing rod. Minutes later, I landed a speckled brook trout not more than six inches long. I landed a few more while working my way slowly around the pond. That's how I found a sweet little spot to spend the night. I retrieved my pack from where I'd dropped it then set up camp.

While propped against a tree and writing in my field journal later on that day, I was startled by the ungodly cry of some creature directly overhead. A woodpecker flopped to the ground shortly thereafter. Naturally I assumed that it was hurt. Then I noticed it was not one but two woodpeckers – male and female – engaging in an act as old as life itself. I smiled knowingly while watching them do their thing, then christened the place 'Pecker Pond in my journal. The forest, as silent and still as it may seem at first, is always full of surprises.

The next day I packed up my things with some reluctance. 'Pecker Pond was such an alluring place that I was tempted to stay another day, but the urge to wander stirred within me. So I tramped along a muddy snowmobile trail that snaked deeper into the woods. I followed it for the better part of the morning, until it no longer took me in the direction that I wanted to go. Then I left the broad trail for a set of bear tracks that meandered over the shoulder of a mountain and into a drainage basin that I wanted to see.

In this new valley I found a small body of water not shown on my map. A family of beavers had dammed the brook, thus creating a pond half the size of a football field. I dropped my pack on high, dry ground then slogged through mud, brush and water just below the beaver dam until I reached the pond's outlet. While crouching behind the dam I snapped my wrist, causing my line to arc towards the middle of the pond. I caught a brook trout right away. Several unsuspecting trout, eight to nine inches long, landed in my lap during the next half hour. Eventually the rest of the pond's residents grew wise to me. The tugs on my line ceased. No matter. A rusty blackbird called out from the top of a dead tree nearby, causing a wave of wild elation to surge through me. It was something I hadn't felt since leaving the Alaskan bush the summer before. Back in my element once again. I named the place Wilderness Pond because it was as deep into the woods as I could get in this corner of Groton State Forest. It reminded me of other, wilder places I had been.

Returning to my pack, I shouldered it then commenced the long tramp back towards the lowlands. Along the way, I stumbled upon a single antler shed by a bull moose. It was half eaten by mice. The antler was just lying there on the forest floor waiting for someone like me to come along and pick it up. I thought about carrying out the trophy but decided against that. Leave it for the hungry. I already had the only thing I really needed from this forest: a link to my own wildness reestablished.

I spent the second night camped along the roaring stream, about halfway between Wilderness Pond and the nearest logging road. I did a little fishing at dusk but spent the better part of the evening just sitting before a small campfire, feeding thumb-sized sticks into the flames, letting my mind wander. I thought about Alaska, where I was now, and every other wild place I'd ever visited. Then I wondered what it is about the wild that I need so badly and tried to guess how many other people felt the same way.

Once the campfire had died down to a handful of embers, I realized that I was a rare bird, indeed, to come out here alone like this. Yet there must be something about wildness that sustains the human race as a whole. Surely everyone must feel the urge to wildness at one point or another during his or her life. Most would call this urge something else, but by any name it remains an unmitigated desire to be oneself without reserve, and to fully engage the world that way. I've reached this same conclusion on other occasions, while sitting alone in front of other campfires. Time and time again I keep coming back to it. Intuitively I know it is true. But rationally speaking, I can't prove it. A claim like this is impossible to prove. Who can say with any certainty what stirs in the hearts of others?

To wander, to wonder. For me the two have always been inextricably entwined. I studied philosophy back in college, eventually taking a degree in the subject, but my wondering began at a much earlier age. It began when I was only ten years old, when I first started to roam about freely.

In the mid-1960s, my family had moved into a house that Dad built in a brand new suburb on the edge of Columbus, Ohio. The back yard abutted a large woodlot. I often went in there to play. Beyond that woodlot, there was a farmer's fallow field slowly returning to the wild. Beyond that, another woodlot, and so on. I explored this countryside, venturing out a little farther each time, making rudimentary maps so that I could find my way home. The more I ventured out, the more I started thinking about things: why some birds leave their feathers on the ground, why rabbits live in dense, thorny thickets, and how thick the ice crusting over tiny streams has to be to support my weight. I thought about early explorers and imagined myself being one. I made primitive shelters as most boys do. I wondered what it would be like to spend a night alone in the woods and whether or not some bogeyman would get me if I did. I wondered about a lot of things. It couldn't be helped.

The more I wandered, the more I wondered. It was so liberating that I wondered if it was a bad thing to roam freely like this. I suspected that the priests and nuns at school would tell me it was a sin if I confessed my wanderings to them. Surely it was illegal, as the occasional "No Trespassing" sign indicated. So I never really told anyone how far out I ranged – not even my parents. And whenever I stumbled by mistake into someone's backyard, I always turned away.

The habit continued into my early teens, after my family moved to a small factory town called Newark. I learned basic backwoods skills in Boy Scouts, and started slipping out of town using creeks as escape routes. By the time I was thirteen, I was taking bike hikes to neighboring towns with my friends – a more social manifestation of the same urge. But I preferred to wander the woodlots on foot alone. That way my mind could wander as well.

In my mid-teens, I lived two lives: a highly social one in town with my buddies and girlfriends, and a solitary one in the fields and woodlots. These two worlds overlapped a bit, but I kept them separate for the most part. My deepest thoughts came when I was alone in the countryside. It's a habit I carried into adulthood, gradually ranging deeper and deeper into the wild. When I was twenty-four, I spent five days alone in the Cascade Mountains of Oregon, in a place called the Three Sisters Wilderness. There I roamed aimlessly through alpine meadows, wetlands and woods feeling more and more at home in the natural world until I sensed the presence of something divine in it. A dozen years later, I had a bush pilot drop me in the wilds of Alaska and that completed the transformation. I emerged from the Alaskan bush an unrepentant woods wanderer. And I've been that way ever since.

To wander you have to let go. To wonder is the same thing. Conventional thinking, like a broad trail cutting through the woods, takes you where you are supposed to go, to an established point of view. Deviation from it only leads to trouble, or so we are led to believe. Madness and going astray. One is mental; the other is physical. They both lead to trouble. That's what people who always stay on the beaten path will tell you, anyhow. But those who allow themselves think differently know otherwise. To have a truly original thought, one has to go where there are no trails. One has to mentally bushwhack.

A few years ago, I stumbled upon a grey squirrel in its death throes. "What's wrong with it?" I thought at first, wondering if there was something I could do that would help the creature get back on its feet again. Then I stepped back in horror, all too aware of what I was witnessing: the fate of us all. I looked to the surrounding treetops to see if there were any winged opportunists up there, waiting for an easy meal. If nothing else, I would stand guard and let this little fellow die in peace. Then I took another step back, realizing that this noble sentiment of mine couldn't change the nature of things. Not really. Nor did I want it to. All the same, it was hard to leave that dying squirrel alone. It was hard not intervening. In my gut I wanted to make wild nature a better, more *humane* place.

As I walked away from the dying squirrel, I thought about Nature with a capital "N" and where creatures like that squirrel and me fit into it. In his book, *The Island Within*, Richard Nelson wrote about the fecundity implicit in nature and asked: "Why this balance, I wonder, this precious gift of life given only at the unthinkable cost of death?" My train of thought ran along a similar track: Why must all living things suffer and die? What is all this living and dying about, anyway? To what end? What purpose does it serve? Surely the nuns who taught me catechism when I was ten years old would not have approved of these thoughts. They would have told me that no one knows the mind of God and we have no business questioning such things. But when I'm alone in the woods, questions like these come all too easily to me. And I don't resist them. I don't resist them because pondering such matters makes me *more* aware of the divine hand at work in the world, not less.

On the third day of my springtime tramp through Groton State Forest, I broke camp and walked downstream until I reached a tributary rushing in from the north. I followed it until I reached yet another pond. This one had primitive campsites on it. There I picked up a track deeply rutted by jeeps or pickup trucks. It connected to the network of logging roads that I'd left a couple days earlier. Back on the road grid again, I felt an immediate shift in my frame of mind. Off the grid, there was the constant danger of being lost, or of falling down injured and not being found. Back on the grid, I felt safe again.

So it goes every time I venture alone into the woods. What is lost by it? What is gained? The way I see it, there are two kinds of people in the world: those who occasionally wander, and those who always follow the straight-and-narrow path. In other words, there are those in touch with their wildness and those who are not. I suppose there is an outlaw aspect to all woods wandering, but that's not what it feels like when I'm doing it. Instead it feels more like freedom. Some call it the freedom of the hills. Free to move around, free to explore the world in which we live, free to think. Free to wonder while wandering. And it all comes so naturally.

Woodpecker

A downy woodpecker
gleans the calf-bone
of a deer. The hungry
winter bird swings
its head repeatedly –
a circus clown juggling
for the crowd, a stranger
glancing to field or grove
for possible dangers
swirling from the snow,
a striped survivor
picking shreds of meat
from whitening bone.

— Walt Franklin

Contributors

Richard Aston has worked as an engineering professor and researcher. He has produced an eclectic array of publications, from engineering textbooks to *Valley Voices*, a collection of poetry released by Foothills Publishing in 2012. His essay "Images of the Deep Anthracite Miner" appeared in *Torch Magazine* last year.

Stuart Bartow teaches writing and literature at SUNY Adirondack. He is also chair of the Battenkill Conservancy, a grassroots environmental group. He has several volumes of poetry in print, along with the non-fiction work, *Teaching Trout to Talk: the Zen of Small Stream Fly Fishing* (RA Press, 2014*)*. He lives near the Vermont-New York border.

Alan Caseline has been a poet, editor and small press publisher for 40 years. He has written and published a number of poetry collections, including *64 Changes* (Foothills Publishing, 2015). He is the editor of a longstanding magazine of watershed poetics, art, and nonfiction called *Rootdrinker*, and as well as an anthology of the Normanskill watershed of upstate New York. Check out his website: rootdrinker.com.

Alan Catlin's verse has appeared in hundreds of literary magazines since the mid-seventies. He has many books and chapbooks of poetry in print, including the newly released, *Walking Among Tombstones in the Fog* (Presa Press, 2017).

He is also editor of an online periodical, *Misfit Magazine*. He lives in Schenectady, New York.

David Cavanagh has had three books of verse published by Salmon Poetry in Ireland: *The Middleman*, *Falling Body* and *Straddle*, and one by Fomite Press: *Cycling in Plato's Cave*. Wood Thrush Books published a chapbook of his poems back in the 1980s. He teaches English at Johnson State College and lives in Burlington, Vermont.

Susan Cohen is the author of two chapbooks as well as two full-length collections of poetry: *Throat Singing* (WordTech, 2012), and *A Different Wakeful Animal,* which won the 2015 Meadowhawk Prize from Red Dragonfly Press. She lives in California.

Tony Cosier is a retired high school teacher who lives in Ottawa, Ontario with his wife, Janet. He is a widely published Canadian poet who has a novel and several plays in print in addition to ten collections of poetry, including *Carillonneur* (Penumbtra Press, 2012).

Walt Franklin is a passionate environmentalist who has done considerable stream restoration work. He has had three essay collections published by Wood Thrush Books: *Beautiful Like a Mayfly, River's Edge* and *Letters from Susquehannock*. He has also written and published many volumes of poetry, including *Earthstars, Chanterelles, Destroying Angles* released by Foothills Publishing in 2016. He writes, teaches and fly-fishes in upstate New York. Check out his blog site: rivertoprambles.wordpress.com.

Gene Grabiner's chapbook, *There Must Be More Than Trigonometry*, was published in 2017 by Foothills Publishing. His poems have appeared in various journals including *Comstock Review*, *Connecticut River Review*, *Jewish Currents*, *Rosebud* and *Slant*. He is a SUNY Distinguished Service Professor Emeritus, and lives in Buffalo, New York.

Vicki Graham is a professor emeritus of English, Creative Writing and Environmental Studies at the University of Minnesota, Morris. She splits her time between Oregon and Minnesota. She has been a writer in residence at the H. J. Andrews Experimental Forest, and a writer/witness of clear cutting at Shotpouch Creek as part of Oregon State University's Spring Creek Project. She has authored *The Hummingbird's Tongue* (Red Dragonfly Press, 2014) along with two other collections of poetry.

Benjamin Green is a writer, artist, and fly fisherman hailing from northern California. He has written several books of prose, including the hiking narrative *Barbless Hooks and Anchorholds,* published by Wood Thrush Books back in 2004, and a more recent collection of self-published essays, *Until Only Silence Remains*. He has written and published several volumes of poetry as well. He is a licensed water treatment operator.

Diane Jarvenpa is the author of several collections of poetry, including *The Tender Wild Things* (New Rivers Press), which received the Midwest Independent Publishers Association book award in poetry. She is also a singer-songwriter who records under the name Diane Jarvi.

Michael Jewell is a poet, painter and novelist living in Calais, Vermont. Two of his poetry chapbooks, *The Power of Wind* and *World Without Edge*, were published by Wood Thrush Books in the 80s and 90s. His verse has appeared in various literary magazines.

Scott King is the author of *All Graced in Green, Leftover Ordinary, Rice County Odonata Journal* and several other volumes of poetry and prose. He is also the editor and publisher of Red Dragonfly Press, and does fieldwork in the study of Minnesota's dragonflies. Check out his website: reddragonflypress.org.

Freya Manfred is a longtime Midwesterner who has lived on both coasts. Her poetry has appeared in over 100 reviews and magazines, and over 40 anthologies. *Speak Mother* (Red Dragonfly Press) is her 8th collection of poetry. Go to freyamanfredwriter.com to see her memoirs, *Frederick Manfred: A Daughter Remembers* and *Raising Twins: A True Life Adventure*.

Karen McKinnon was a Poet in the Schools for the National Endowment For the Arts, and Poet-in-Residence at the Wurlitzer Foundation in Taos, New Mexico. Her work is included in the anthology *In Company: An Anthology of New Mexico Poets after 1960* (University of New Mexico Press, 2004).

Walt McLaughlin is the editor and publisher of Wood Thrush Books. He has a dozen books in print, including a narrative about hiking in the Adirondacks, *The Allure of*

Deeps Woods, and a recently published collection of essays, *Cultivating the Wildness Within*.

Howard Nelson is a poet and semi-retired professor of English who lives in the Finger Lakes region of New York. *All the Earthly Lovers: Selected & New Poems* is his most recent book of verse. He is also the editor of the book *Earth, My Likeness: Nature Poetry of Walt Whitman* published by North Atlantic Books in 2010. Visit his website: howardneslonpoet.com.

Helen Ruggieri taught at the University of Pittsburgh, Bradford, PA for 20 years and now teaches a poetry workshop in Olean, New York where she lives. She has several volumes of poetry in print including *The Kingdom Where No One Keeps Time*. She is also the editor of *Written on Water*, an anthology of writings on the Allegheny River published by Mayapple Press in 2013.

Jeanne Shannon is the editor/publisher of The Wildflower Press in addition to being a memoirist, fiction writer and poet. Her most recent collection of poetry, *Summoning*, was released by Mercury HeartLink in 2015. Check out her author's page at Amazon.com.

t. kilgore splake escaped academia in his 50s to live in Michigan's upper peninsula and focus on his poetry and photography. He is a widely published poet who has penned over 75 books. His most recent collection of poetry is *Last Dance* (Transcendant Zero Press, 2017). Check out his author's page at Amazon.com.

William Weiss is a retired Professor of English now focusing on his writing and artwork. His most recent book is a collection of essays and experimental fiction, *Orbiting William S Burroughs*, released in 2015. He currently lives in upstate New York with his wife Susan, but they will soon be moving out west.

Clarence Wolfshohl has been active in the small press world as a writer and publisher for nearly fifty years. He has published poetry and non-fiction in many journals, both print and online. In 2016, Virtual Artists Collective published his e-chapbook, *Scattering Ashes*. Wolfshohl lives in the suburbs of Toledo, Missouri with his dog and cat.